Reaching the Heart and Mind of Muslims

Matthew Stone

D1711877

1

Dedication

I dedicate this book to my wife and daughters who listened to me talk about it for hours on end. They even graciously smiled and pretended to be interested.

To my many Jewish, Muslim, Christian, and atheist friends who have taught me so much about how to be a committed person of faith and how to love those whose faith differs from mine.

To my friends at Columbia International University—Warren Larson, Trevor Castor, Steve Farra, Rhonda Pruitt, and many others.

To my students who read the book when it was in very rough draft form.

To you, the reader.

Table of Contents

Chapter 1--Introduction

Indiana Jones: "Get back to Cairo, get us some transport to England. Boat, plane, anything... Meet me at Omar's. Be ready for me; I'm going after that truck."
Sallah: "How?"
Indiana Jones: "I don't know. I'm making this up as I go.

    I have taught Muslims studies for about 20 years, and during that time a student invariably asks, "What do you think is the best way to reach out to Muslims?" or "What model do you like best for reaching Muslims?" I never know quite what to say because I don't think in those terms. So I usually mutter, somewhat tongue in cheek, something such as "I like the Raiders of the Lost Arc approach." I then proceed to relate to them the conversation between Indiana Jones and Sallah written at the top of this page. In the scene, Indiana Jones and Sallah were in a very tense situation and Sallah wanted to know what they should do next. It was at that point that Indiana Jones said, "I don't know. I'm making this up as I go." Sure, I am joking when I say this to my sincere students, but at the same time I am not completely joking.

    I am joking because the fact is that I have spent years studying Muslims, Islam, and interacting with Muslims in all kinds of settings. Thus I do have considerable knowledge about these matters. I am not totally just making it up as I go along. On the other hand, there is a sense in which every Muslim is different and every situation is different; consequently, there is always an element of "not knowing" in each encounter with a Muslim. So I am in the curious position of knowing and not knowing at the same time.

    For many people "not knowing" is an uncomfortable state of being, so they look for structure, a model, the "right" way, a step-by-step manual in an effort to make an ambiguous situation seem unambiguous. They want to know exactly what to do, when. That is natural and normal for many of us. The problem is that when we believe that we can't stand ambiguity, we start avoiding the people and situations about which we make us anxious. The result is that we tend to avoid the messy realities of life. Sometimes the avoidance ends up having us avoid the Muslims around us and retreat into a world of our own beliefs about Muslims. Another way that avoiding ambiguity gets manifested is in a tendency within some people to declare something that is not absolute, an absolute. Stated differently, we seem to have a tendency to confuse our pictures of reality for the reality itself because doing so is easy and reduces the anxiety in the midst of the ambiguity of reality.

Models are helpful, in the same way that habits are helpful. They both allow us to navigate through new and sometimes confusing situations without always starting at ground zero. Models are like maps where map are pictures, simplified pictures or representations of territory. They are condensed and accessed when we need them. However, maps are not territory. Some maps are good maps and help us steer through geography without too many problems. Some maps aren't quite so good and end up having us go down paths with dead ends or venturing into dangerous territory. Models can be helpful, but they should never be confused with territory itself. Maps can never give one the feel of the land, its uniqueness, its smells, and its sounds. If we focus exclusively on the map and not the territory, we miss the richness of the land.

Models for reaching Muslims are also maps. They aren't necessarily bad, but they are not a replacement for experiencing individual Muslims and the richness of their culture, groups, families, and individuality. Models of missions are helpful when viewed in a big brush stroke kind of way, but they are not helpful to the degree that they get in the way by having us focus too much on the model and too little on the uniqueness of the Muslim right in front of us. Too many Christians place their faith in the map and devote too much time arguing with other Christians about why their map is the best map.

In this book, I will be looking at how we can experience Muslims in their uniqueness. I will try to avoid reducing individual Muslims to mere examples of types.

It is certainly not an original stance, but I shy away from talking about 'Islam' and 'Muslims', and instead, try to refer to "Whose Islam" and "Which Muslim." I shy away from questions such as "What does the Qur'an say about..." Instead, I focus on what this individual Muslim believes about this particular verse in the Qur'an, and so forth. In 1988 Alisdair MacIntyre wrote a book entitled, Whose Justice? Which Rationality? I guess in this book I am asking, "Whose Islam? Which Muslim?" Extend this approach to include, "Whose Muhammad? Which Shari'ah?"

Clearly, only one historical Muhammad existed. Despite that fact, I encourage you to pick up some of the existing books on the life and person of Muhammad. What you get are multiple maps or pictures of Muhammad, and some of the aspects of those pictures are widely divergent, even when Muslims are the creators of those pictures. For example, consider 23 Years by Ali Dashti, a liberal Shi'a Muslim who was critical of what he took to be the myths used by Muslim biographers of Muhammad to describe the life of Muhammad. Contrast this with The Life of Muhammad, a biography of Muhammad by Haykal, a conservative Sunni Muslim whose biography of Muhammad is filled with what Dashti would simply dismiss as myth but which Haykal appeals to modern science to interpret and justify. Finally consider the biography of Muhammad written by Martin Lings, a British convert to Islam and a Sufi whose picture of Muhammad embraces an appreciation for what Dashti would reject outright but far richer than the more ossified version Muhammad's biography written by Haykal. Even some Christian writers see a significant difference between the Muhammad of Mecca and the Muhammad of Medina. Which picture of Muhammad is the "real" picture? That is not for me to say, but something of deep passion for many Muslims.

While it is helpful to understand believing Muslims and their cultural identities, we need to be cautious about talking too

7

globally about "The Muslim Mind" or "The Arab Muslim."
Muslims are not products of cultural factories; Arabs are not all
the same. Understanding someone's culture is tremendously
helpful in understanding an individual, but I shy away from
embracing cultural determinism that glosses over differences and
can, in its worse form, view individuals merely as an expression
of culture.

In philosophy a distinction is made between essentialism
and nominalism. The difference between these views is whether
one tends to see abstractions as "really real" and assign a lesser
place to individual or particular existing things (a view called
essentialism), or whether one focuses on individual existing things
and sees abstractions as ideas or words whose use is helpful for
communicating but that those words and ideas are not as fully real
as individual things (a view called nominalism). I realize that this
distinction sounds abstract and perhaps not useful to the topic at
hand. However it is relevant because the view one has about
reality largely determines how one sees Muslims and interacts
with them. If you tend to see Islam as the primary reality and
groups of Muslims as somehow participating in that larger reality,
you tend toward essentialism. You might be predisposed to
expend your energy trying to get at the "essence of the true Islam"
and its message, try to understand "the Muslim mind" or "Arabs,"
etc. If you see particular expressions of religious beliefs and
practices of Muslims as primary and view Islam as merely a term
that is helpful to communicate with others, you tend toward
nominalism. You might then try to study specific beliefs of
particular Muslims, the diversity of expressions of Muslims as
they live and believe, the multiple interpretations of the Qur'an
and Sunnah (the life example of Muhammad as captured in the
hadith), etc.

I tend toward nominalism, less for metaphysical reasons
and more for pragmatic reasons. When we think that Islam is the
"really real", we tend to lump Muslims together and blur
diversity. We tend to say things such as "Islam teaches...," or
"There is something in the essence of Islam that gives rise to

8

terrorism," "If Muslims truly understand the Qur'an, then they will be violent," or "Islam is an aggressive religion. " Essentialism tends toward "all" and "none," "always," and "never," whereas nominalism tends toward "some," "many," or "a majority." Nominalism is more qualified, less absolute. In the extreme, essentialism gives rise to or supports prejudice and bias. I prefer nominalism despite the fact that it is more ambiguous, messier, and harder to reduce to "a" model or a single strategy. I, however, work hard to avoid being a nominalist who has simply despaired of finding trends and similarities to live in a world of mere unique entities without commonalities. It is a fine line to walk that requires humility, ongoing dialogue with a community of believers and scholars, and ongoing curiosity about me and my biases.

I have doctorates in philosophy and psychology, but please don't be too quick to dismiss my ideas. My educational training shapes how I view Muslims and interacting with them. My philosophical studies and my experience teaching rhetorical theory, especially modern rhetorical theory as set forth by Stephen Toulmin, impact how I think about argument and the nature of persuasive conversations with others. Philosophy is to a large degree about argument and what makes an argument valid and sound. So, of course, I have been fascinated by the apologetics of Christians and Muslims in their interaction with each other. As a philosopher I am curious about the "bad" arguments both present to "the other" to describe their own faith and to critique the other's faith. However, rhetorical theory has made me keenly interested in what makes an argument persuasive and how Muslims and Christians may offer valid or sound arguments in ways that fall flat or fail to influence in a desired way the intended audience. Finally, as a student of psychology, I am quite curious about the emotional dimension of human interaction, in this case, Christian-Muslim interaction and the psychology of persuasion. So my approach in this book to interacting with Muslims is informed by those disciplines, not to come up with "a" model, but rather to consider ways in which to share one's faith logically,

9

effectively, and with emotional depth while accepting the uniqueness of the Muslims in our lives and to do so in ways that are loving, respectful, and embrace the intrinsic value of the individual Muslim. There is someone else in whom I am interested--you. I am interested in how your thoughts and beliefs impact your interaction with Muslims such that you experience emotions that are not helpful or that sabotage you in reaching out to Muslims. How do you make yourself anxious, angry, or highly frustrated in those interactions? What gets you derailed and overly-focused on winning an argument rather than staying curious and loving in your interaction? Why do you cling to a given model even when evidence suggests that there is a downside to doing so? How much is confirmatory bias at work in you, namely, do you have some general beliefs about Muslims and then you tend only to focus on those aspects of your interactions with Muslims that confirm that bias and have you end up saying to yourself, "See, all Muslims are that way."

You are not going to agree with everything I say in this short book. I am fine with that. My goal is to explore the ways in which we Christians interact with Muslims and the pitfalls in doing so. My goal is also to think seriously about how we can be in relationships with Muslims that are loving, respectful, and avoid manipulation or deception. I am only one voice in this discussion. I will consider other approaches that differ significantly with how I do things. Beneath it all, my goal is to act out of a love for Christ, be open and informed by the ways in which He interacted with others, and to enter into the lives of Muslims with the same love Christ had for others. My belief is that all hearts cry out for the living God whether Christian heart, Muslim heart, Buddhist heart, Jewish heart, or atheist heart. Whether we realize it or not, the rightful and natural object of our deepest desire is God as witnessed to and seen in the person and life of Jesus.

Chapter 2--Argument

...and you shall love the Lord your God with all your heart, and with all your soul, and with all your mind, and with all your strength. Gospel of Mark 12:30

This chapter is about argument in the broadest sense. Many people who interact with Muslims think that argument is the most important way to interact with them. They may be using the word 'argument' differently than I am. The word 'argument' often connotes a fight, quarrel, debate, angry interchange, or the like. That is not how I am using the term. Instead, I am talking about either an explicit or implicit process in which two or more people are seeking a solution to a question or problem, i.e., it is an attempt to persuade someone about something. An explicit argument involves claims and attempts to support the claims with reason and evidence. An implicit argument may not state the claim and support but instead attempts to persuade an audience through a visual, such as a bumper sticker, T-shirt, picture, etc. (Ramage, Bean, & Johnson, 2010)

Argument assumes truth seeking and persuasion, and always involves an audience. My emphasis will be on truth seeking more than winning an argument, but persuasion is a necessary component of an argument. Thus argument is not a sterile statement of claim and supporting reasons and evidence. An audience is essential to how I am using the term and the form that arguments ought to take if they are to be effective with the intended audience.

Every argument has a content, structure, and goal. The content is comprised of the statements or words in the argument. The structure is how those statements and words are arranged; and the goal is to persuade an audience. Effective arguments appeal to an audience in particular ways and at times using a combination of ways. Traditionally those persuasive appeals were called the logos, pathos, and ethos of an argument. Those appeals exist within a context that has been called and illustrated as the rhetorical triangle. The three points of the triangle could be labeled the message, the writer/speaker, and the audience. So a writer or speaker is trying to persuade an audience by presenting a message in a persuasive way appealing to logos, pathos, and ethos.

The logos of the message focuses on the logicality of the message, i.e., the consistency of the content, the clarity of the message, and the logical connections between the claims and the support offered for the claims.

The ethos focuses on the character of the writer or speaker as projected by the message. Does the writer/speaker use a believable tone or style? Does she/he consider alternative views? Does the writer/speaker seem honest, trustworthy, or credible?

Pathos focuses on the values, beliefs, and emotions of the intended audience. While logos may appeal to the mind of the audience, the pathos of the argument appeals to the audience's emotions, imagination, and feelings.

Some people say that there is another kind of appeal of an argument that should be considered—the kairos. Kairos focuses on the timing of the argument. Is it the right moment to offer this argument? Is my audience ready to hear this message at this time and in this way? Should I wait or change my timing?

There are many ways to put all this together. Aristotle and classical philosophers did it through formal logic. That is one approach and while it is strong on considerations of logos, can fail to consider the audience. Toulmin, a contemporary philosopher, developed another way to talk about these matters that very much considers the audience.

Apologetics has typically been approached through a classical formal logical approach and while this approach is strong on logos it often doesn't fully consider the fact that the goal is persuasion of an audience, and audiences are composed of flesh and blood people, not disembodied minds. Audiences are moved by values, feelings, and how the writer/speaker comes across to the audience. Therefore, in this book, I will appeal more to

Toulmin's audience-friendly approach, looking also at some findings of the psychology of influence.

Logos: Be logical!

When you hear a Muslim's argument to persuade you to become a Muslim, or when you set forth an argument to persuade a Muslim, think about the bottom line claim that is being made and what would logically support that claim. When those two elements are put together in one statement connected by the word 'because,' it is called an enthymeme. So the structure of an enthymeme is: claim + 'because' + reason. An example is, "The Qur'an is a miracle of Muhammad because he was illiterate." Another example is, "Jesus is the unique Son of God because He was conceived by the Holy Spirit and resurrected after being crucified to death."

Of course, there is more to an argument than just offering an enthymeme. However, if you become aware of the basic enthymeme of an argument, you will be focused on the core of the argument and minimize the possibility of getting lost in the words and end up muddying your goal. An enthymeme needs to be developed to be persuasive. To understand the parts of the argument to be developed, we need to learn some new terms: warrant, grounds, and backing.

A warrant is an assumption that an audience needs to accept for the argument to be appealing or acceptable to the audience. Often a writer or speaker is not conscious of her/his assumptions and whether the audience would even find the assumptions persuasive or acceptable.

For example, consider the enthymeme previously mentioned, "The Qur'an is a miracle of Muhammad because Muhammad was illiterate." While not explicitly stated in the argument, an unwritten assumption is that for something to have the excellent literary quality of the Qur'an and come from an illiterate, a miracle must have taken place. Some people might find this a persuasive assumption, but others might think that high literary quality could come from someone with excellent literary

13

talent devoid of the ability to read or write. Thus they wouldn't acknowledge that the talent was the product of a miracle.

It is very important that Christians become aware of their assumptions when offering an argument to Muslims. For example, I have often heard Christians argue, "Jesus was either the Lord, a liar, or a lunatic when he claimed to be the Lord. Since there is no evidence that he was a liar or lunatic, he must be the Lord." This argument is rarely persuasive to a Muslim because it has a warrant, or assumption, that isn't persuasive to most Muslims, namely, that the Bible is even reliable enough to be used to determine exactly what Jesus actually claimed about him. Later we will look at some reasons why Muslims reject this warrant/assumption, but for now I hope you can see that if a Muslim doesn't accept the warrant, the argument will not be persuasive. It would be wise for the Christian to think deeply and clearly about possible acceptable warrants.

Grounds and backing are also important. Grounds are the evidence that a writer/speaker offers to help the audience accept the reason(s) offered in support of the claim. For example, if a Christian argued that Jesus is the Lord because He resurrected from the dead, the grounds supporting the claim might be biblical textual evidence such as more than 500 witnesses saw Jesus alive after his death, four separate Gospel accounts are consistent on the resurrection of Jesus, etc. So in this particular argument, the grounds are testimonial in nature.

Backing becomes important the more doubtful an audience is about the writer/speaker's warrants or assumptions. I once met a philosophy professor who walked out of an Easter service at a church. He was disgusted by the preacher's "argument for the resurrection." When I asked him what his problem was with the preacher's argument, he said that the preacher failed to state his assumptions as well as the reasons for someone to accept his assumptions. What the professor wanted was both the preacher's warrant and reasons underlying the warrant, namely, the backing of the argument. I could have told him that the preacher's assumption was that the Bible was a reliable source for the belief

14

that there were 500 witnesses to the resurrection of Jesus. I knew this would not be a warrant accepted by the professor. He would want to know the reasons why this warrant is believable. I told him that the preacher never offered such a backing because it was accepted by his audience without stating it. I sympathized with the professor and said that setting forth that backing would certainly be called for if the preacher were to talk to him, the professor. We then set up a series of meetings to discuss just what would constitute an adequate backing for the warrant. The point is, the less likely an audience is to accept your assumptions, the more important it is to set forth your backing. For most Muslim to hear a Christian utter, "the Bible says" isn't going to be persuasive.

Ethos: Be believable!

If an audience doesn't believe you, you are not going to be persuasive to that audience. I have met Christians who said that ultimately it is the Holy Spirit who determines whether someone accepts an argument or not. True, but this truth does not give a speaker/writer permission to be rude, sloppy, unfair, or a poor witness to the grace of God. God uses people and their traits to get arguments across to others, so the characteristics of the speaker/writer are important. The last thing we would want to do is package the truth in a totally unattractive wrapping. So, how can you maximize your credibility to a Muslim audience?

Know what you are talking about. You don't have to be a biblical scholar or theologian, but know the basics of your faith. One area in which you are an expert is the effect on your life of embracing the faith. If you don't know something about the Bible or an article of faith, offer to look into it, or arrange a meeting with someone who does have an answer (and an engaging personality).

Be fair. Sure you need to know the basics of your faith, but when you touch on the faith of a Muslim, demonstrate that you are fairly presenting their views in a courteous way. Better yet, refrain from telling a Muslim what Muslims believe or what the Qur'an teaches. Have the Muslim tell you what she/he believes. If it is a lecture setting with many Muslims listening to you, try starting with questions to get Muslim views on the topic. Listening shows that you are courteous and taking them and their views seriously. If you are writing, quote Muslim sources rather than Christian ones. This can be challenging if you strongly disagree with Islamic ideas such as the following:

+The Bible has been corrupted
+The Trinity is a false doctrine
+Jesus was never crucified
+The Bible predicts the coming of Muhammad after Jesus.

Build a bridge. Starting with shared beliefs and assumptions is more helpful than beginning with differences. Sure, eventually differences need to be addressed, but rarely is it helpful to begin there. Remember, bridges go from one side to another. The purpose of building bridges is to advance an argument and help the Muslim move toward Christ. This is often difficult because fellow Christians may want you to crush the false beliefs of Muslims right at the beginning of your interaction. Some Muslims want to show the inadequacy of your views right from the beginning. Building bridges can be tough. One friend of mine says that when you try to be a bridge, you get stepped on from both sides. True, but that doesn't invalidate the value of the bridge. What are beliefs held in common by most Christians and Muslims?

+Jesus is a prophet
+Jesus will return as the Messiah
+There is a God
+What we believe matters
+What we do in this life matters
+Sharing one's faith is important
+People have intrinsic value

Remember, these are bridge topics at the beginning of an interaction and are just one side of the bridge, but as we cross the bridge together, the topics change—and ideally our relationship will change, growing in depth and love and trust.

An area of psychology I find fascinating is the psychology of influence or persuasion. Even if we think of reaching Muslims through argument, rhetorical theory recognizes that the goal of argument is to persuade people to embrace the truth. Persuasion is influence. Let's consider some of the findings in the psychology of influence and their potential for reaching Muslims. I want to focus primarily on the features or characteristics of the speaker/writer that are persuasive.

Cialdini (1993) describes a simple rule, "We most prefer to say 'yes' to the request of someone we know and like" (p.167). Charitable organizations often recruit volunteers to seek donations in the community or neighborhood from which they want donations. Why? It is an instance of the rule just mentioned. Now, while persuading someone to come to the Lord is not the same as asking for a donation, the rule is still relevant. We have a greater chance of successfully witnessing to someone we know and with whom we associate regularly. It is clear. Mingle! Get out of your house; get to know your neighbors; go to where Muslims are. You might try some of the following locations as places to connect with Muslims:

+**Halal stores.** Halal is the equivalent of kosher. Halal foods are foods that are permissible for Muslims to eat. For example, some Muslims only want to eat meat slaughtered in an "Islamically permissible" way and most want to avoid pork and alcohol. They can get such permissible food at a halal shop. I frequently go to a halal shop, not only because it is a great place to meet Muslims, but I can find some great food.

+**Mosques or Islamic centers.** Friday, sometime around noon or shortly thereafter, is a special day of community worship; so many Muslims are present at the mosque on that day. A more relaxed day to meet Muslims is on a Saturday or Sunday. Often Muslims teach classes for the children and adults in a Muslim "Sunday School." They often serve food and enjoy each other's company. Sometimes these Sunday events are held in public schools or in churches when there is no mosque in the vicinity. I have made some great Muslim friends in such settings.

+**Ethnic organizations.** Some ethnic organizations have Muslims as members, such as Arab, Pakistani, Indian, Turkish, or Iranian organizations. These can be great locations in which to meet Muslims.

+**Common grounds.** Volunteering with Muslims on projects or in causes of common interest, such as clean up the community project, getting rid of sex shops from neighborhoods, etc., can be great settings to meet Muslims. Muslims are often very interested in issues of ethics and morality and would appreciate working with Christians with similar sympathies.

+**ESL class.** Try volunteering with an English as a Second Language (ESL) program or class. Some ESL programs like to pair Muslims with native speakers of English so the students get practice speaking English. I have done this and through this I have met a Muslim man who became one of my best friends. While he is still a Muslim, he has been a great advocate, telling Muslims they are confused about what Christians really believe. He has said, "I feel like a Christian inside. Something just holds me back." I enjoy being his friend and answering the questions he has.

+**School events.** I have a friend who loves meeting Muslims at soccer practice or matches when his children play soccer. It is interesting that in such a setting Muslim parents often share their struggles with their children. It was a topic of common interest. He would often begin asking whether they would mind if he prayed with them right there on the sidelines or in the bleachers. Often they were very open to it and in following weeks he would ask how the situation was and would himself report the changes he saw in his own children—or not! He has been blessed with Muslims calling him and asking him to pray for other matters in their life. And yes, he prays pray in the name of Jesus. They know he is a Christian and that Christians love Jesus and pray in his name. He says that he has never encountered a problem with this.

The bottom line is: Hang out with Muslims! Get to know them, open up and let them know you. Be real, and wonderful things can happen.

We like people who are similar to us. Cialdini (1993) says this is true whether the similarly is "in the area of opinion, personality, traits, background, or life-style" (p. 173). Let me give you an example. I am a Midwest boy. Like a lot of Midwesterners, I am a happy kind of guy—frequently laughing, joking with people, and always curious about people and their stories. I am a curious combination of hard working but also laid back and ready to hang out--productively waste time. Once I gathered a bunch of friends to go to a deli I like. At some point in the meal we shared our backgrounds (these were new friends) and we got a good laugh: all of us were from the Midwest, all but two had the same political leanings, and it just went on and on like that. Like likes like. Now, I am not advocating that we just socialize with clones, but psychology shows that there is a tendency for us to like people who are similar to us in some way.

You may be thinking that this could make hanging out with Muslims difficult because they are so different from us. Look beneath the surface! Some may dress differently, eat slightly different foods, or have a different first language, but there can be surprising ways in which you are similar to a given Muslim. [I am aware that right now I am talking about meeting Muslims in the West, but the same points are relevant to Muslims anywhere in the world. I have had great interactions with Muslims in Muslim populated countries throughout the world.]

Let me give you an example. I am a philosopher and a psychotherapist. Is it a surprise that a number of my friends are Muslim philosophers and psychotherapists? In fact, right now I am working on a project in psychology with a Muslim psychologist. We became friends at a conference on treating adolescents who have ADHD. When we introduced ourselves, I

19

mentioned my interest in Islam and Muslims and she approached me at the break. She was fine, although she is a woman, with collaborating with a Christian man on a research project. She was fascinated how I was so fascinated with Islam. Like likes like.

If you are an engineer, meet some Muslims engineers. If you are a physician, you have a lot of choices. If you are a mom who works in your home and is on the road with all kinds of kids in the SUV, meet Muslim women living that life. If you love soccer, want to learn Middle Eastern cooking, or you want your favorite Republican or Democrat politician to win, connect with likeminded Muslims. It really isn't that hard.

We like people who compliment us. Most of my life I have been too stingy with my compliments of others. However, a few years ago, I changed. Recently, I had dinner with a Muslim who has radically different political views from mine (don't go too far with hanging out with those who are just like you). We were having a fantastic discussion about universal health care and I noticed that beneath our political differences we both wanted people who needed health care to get it and not to have to suffer. I stopped and said, "I really appreciate you. You have opened my eyes to how close minded I have been most of my life. Thanks!" He had a huge smile on his face. Tell Muslims what you appreciate about them. We all like to be valued. Thank them for challenging conversations, their time, and the gift of their presence in your life. You can do this in so many different ways. I often send Muslims cards around major holidays—Christmas, Milad a Nabi (birthday of Muhammad), Easter, Eids, etc. I send them cards for days that are special to me and to them. I can't imagine celebrating a special day, such as Christmas, without including my Muslim friends. They may not get the feel of Christmas and its significance for me, but it is a time I can let them see my joy. They always thank me.

Cialdini (1993) notes a piece of research conducted in the 1930s by a psychologist named Gregory Razran. He coined a phrase "luncheon technique" because the research demonstrated that people become fonder of the people and things they experienced while eating (p. 193). Why do you think that we have the term "fund raising dinner"? I am not advocating that you try to manipulate people with this food association principle, but why not sit with Muslims and share ideas over food. I have invited Muslim friends to Middle Eastern restaurants and ask their advice on what would be good selections. I get their overall rating of the place and we have some great conversations.

It can be trickier sometimes to invite Muslims to your home for food until you learn how observant they are about the meat they eat. Just ask them what you should watch out for. It would be a little easier for me because I don't eat pork, but asking about their customs could result in some interesting conversation and reduce their embarrassment about bringing up the issue for fear of disappointing or offending you. Safe bets are to serve fish, rice, salad (no bacon bits), bread (made without animal shortening), tea, coffee, and fresh fruit. Some Muslims are reluctant to eat baked desserts if they think that we may have used vanilla extract, which contains alcohol, which they may not be around or eat.

Some strict Muslims consider dogs to be unclean, so it can be a challenge if you happen to have a pet dog. For example, if I were to have a Muslim over for dinner, I have a crate for my golden retriever. I hate to put her in the crate, but fortunately she actually likes it and doesn't mind being in it—if I give her treats. I would do the same if some good Christian friends come over and had a child who is afraid of dogs.

If prayer time comes in when Muslims are visiting you, they may be reluctant to pray in rooms with statues, photographs, or pictures of living creatures. Just cover these items or remove them from the room. You can give them a towel on which to pray and place plenty of towels in a nearby bathroom so they can make the necessary ritual ablutions for prayer. It is important not to walk in front of them as they are praying. They appreciate the effort.

Cialdini (1993) cites research that has demonstrated that we seem to be more open to being persuaded by those we deem as an authority or an expert. What factors contribute to someone being perceived as an authority or expert?

+**Titles**: There are all kinds of titles that often, but not invariably, influence us positively—doctor, professor, judge, pastor, Father, imam, etc. These titles are associated with deep relevant learning. Even when people are confused about the title, those who have a title are often elevated in status. I have a doctorate in psychology and can legitimately call myself, "doctor". I will never forget an older lady who came to my office carrying a cottage cheese container. I thought that was a little odd, but I am a psychotherapist, after all. We chatted for a short time, and I then proceeded to get a history and attempted to get a detailed description of her current symptoms that brought her in to see me. She reported no troubling emotional or behavioral symptoms, no apparent psychosis was witnessed, so I kept digging. Sometimes people are just lonely, so I asked her what she hoped to get out of therapy to see whether loneliness might be the issue. At that point I became really confused when she handed me the cottage cheese container. I asked her what it was and she said it was a stool sample. The mystery was solved. I then explained that I was not that kind of doctor, but the halo effect was clearly in place evidenced by what she then said, "Are you sure you can't help me anyway? You are a doctor." Sometimes even when people are confused about the title, the status remains.

Titles demonstrate or suggest specialized knowledge. Don't despair if you used your energy and time to gain knowledge that didn't result in a title. Perhaps you have other titles, such as "senior marketing expert," "mother of five grown children," "fly fishing award winner three years in a row," "lead realtor in number of sales for 2012," etc. Your informal title may carry considerable status in ways you may be unaware. For example, in many Muslim populated countries, mothers have high status. Oh, and don't forget compliments. I compliment Muslims on their titles and the work that went into getting them, especially the title of being a mom or dad to some great children.

+Clothes: I hate to admit that I don't like this area, but for the sake of intellectual honesty I have to cover it. Numerous studies have demonstrated that we tend to be more compliant with requests made by well-dressed individuals. Uniforms are a clear example—police, military, fire fighters, a physician's white coat—uniforms tend to influence, often positively dependent on your life experience.

In interacting with Muslims, modest dress is more persuasive than revealing trendy clothes. Dress appropriately. I tend not to dress to impress (unless I am looking for a job), but I do tend to dress to put others at ease—within reason. On this point, I often have a Christian say, "I shouldn't have to dress to please someone else. It isn't fair." There is no "should" here and perhaps it isn't fair. I think those statements come out of a wrong focus. I try to focus on what is helpful rather than what I am free to do.

I guess the bottom line for me is that there are factors that contribute to us being believable and trustworthy to others. Much of this is cultural, so take some time to study the culture of people with whom you interact. Have them help you learn. Grow in the likeness of Christ so that you also increase the likelihood that you will be likeable. I deplore it when people—some of them people motivated purely out of love for money—use this information to manipulate us to be superficial consumers. I would hope that my motivation is to show respect to others and that I take the moral responsibility to honor the psychology given to us by God to draw us closer to each other and glorify God. Pray for purity of intentionality. Give others you trust the permission to let you know when they are uncomfortable with the ways in which you use your knowledge.

Pathos: Touch emotions!

Did you ever see Star Trek? What did you think of the character, Spock? I am always impressed by his logic, but I always have the feeling that I could only take him in small doses because at some point I like to relate to someone who demonstrates some emotion. It is human to be excited, bored, sad, joyful, frustrated, annoyed, calm, fulfilled, etc. God created us with emotions. Sure we can use them wrongly and they can make a needless mess of our life, but helpful emotions connect us to others and can help us enjoy life and be more productive in it. We tend to be moved by emotions that we see in others.

Ramage, Bean, & Johnson (2007) note ways in which one can touch the emotions of one's audience in the context of an argument:

+**Be as concrete as possible**. Think about driving down the highway when you are very hungry. If you see a sign that says "Food" not much comes to mind. You don't know what kind of food you will find at the next exit and not much emotion is activated. However, if the sign read, "Fast food" a clearer picture would come to mind—hamburgers, fried chicken, pizza, tacos, etc. If the sign were to say, "McDonald's" you have an even clearer image—Chicken McNuggets, Big Mac, fries. The more specific or concrete the language, the clearer the image and the greater the possibility of emotion being mobilized—negative or positive. If your argument is philosophically abstract, the smaller the chance of the audience's emotions being touched. So tell stories, use examples, cautiously use analogies.

A word of caution about analogies: I remember when I was not a Christian that some Christians tried to convince me of the logicality or feasibility of the Trinity by appealing to analogies. Not only did the analogies not work with me, but they contributed, I believe, to my view that Christians held their faith for illogical reasons. Some of the analogies that I heard were: +**The Trinity is like an egg**—the three persons in the Trinity are like the shell, yellow, and white of the egg—all different but constituting one egg. For this analogy to have worked for me, the shell would have to be fully the egg, the yellow to be fully the egg, and the white to be fully the egg. I rejected the analogy and thought that the Christians who said it were silly.

+The Trinity is like water—the three persons in the Trinity are like the steam, liquid, and ice, different forms but still water. One of my undergraduate majors was chemistry, so I always told Christians who uttered this analogy that water vapor, liquid, and ice are not equal, they all have different energy levels. Aren't the persons of the Trinity supposed to be equal—equal in holiness, power, and all other attributes? For me the analogy failed. There were too many relevant dissimilarities between the two objects. **+The Trinity is like a person with three different roles**—son, father, and husband, but all three roles are in one person. But wasn't the doctrine of the Trinity about three persons constituting one being, not merely three roles in one person? Again, the analogy didn't work for me.

I am not saying, never to use analogies, but always be ready to acknowledge the relevant dissimilarities between the analogy and the reality to which the analogy points. Think about your audience and don't lose credibility by employing bad examples or analogies. **+Be sure your language is culturally relevant, and avoid cultural taboos.** For example, in some Muslim cultures it wouldn't be appropriate, and it could mobilize negative emotion, to use examples that describe the physical traits of a woman. Even calling God, "Father" can mobilize negative emotions within some Muslims because to many of them it would mean to attribute sexual activity to Allah, which would be repugnant to them. Using humor about important religious figures is common in Western cultures, but not so common in Muslim cultures. It is often not only repugnant to use humor with respect to Muhammad, the prophets, Allah, messengers, the rightly guided caliphs (Abu Bakr, Umar, Uthman, and Ali), Sufi saints, Shi'a imams, but it can lead to deep anger. Again, take the time to learn about the Muslim's culture.

Kairos: Be timely!

In II Corinthians 4, Paul calls negative events a "slight momentary affliction." Paul is correct when we can view the event through the lens of eternity. However, immediately after a major negative event, we have difficulty shifting from the event before our eyes to viewing the event in light of eternity. Can you imagine telling a parent who has just experienced the death of their precious young child that this loss is only a slight momentary affliction? That would be cruel and insensitive, not because it is wrong, but because it is wrong timing, and if your goal is to sooth the parents, then you just failed. It would have been better for you to act as the friends of Job when they just sat silently in the dirt with him—before they opened their mouths and spouted insensitive and unhelpful words designed to correct his thinking.

Opening a discussion about justice within Islamic fiqh (jurisprudence) or kalam (theology) by discussing the deliberate killing of nearly 800 Jews in Medina during the lifetime of Muhammad when you are just starting a relationship with a Muslim, is bad timing. Actual event; bad timing. Think! What is your goal! Do the words that come from your mouth help you move toward that goal? You can be right, but not bright unless you show the light of Christ.

I have met Christians who say that they must boldly tell the truth at the earliest possible time in their interaction with a Muslim. I disagree. If the Muslim experiences the truth as rude or insensitive, you may be right but you are definitely not bright. That is why I tend not to like rules such as "I must always share all the truth right at the beginning," "I must always correct a Muslim's mistaken beliefs about the truths of Christianity as soon as the Muslim utters the mistake," "I must always be assertive with a Muslim and stand up for Christianity." I fully understand wanting to stand on the side of truth. That is noble and not problematical. It is not a matter of whether to stand for the truth, but when and how. Standing on the side of truth is good; standing on the side of truth in the right time and in the right way, is both good and wise. Unfortunately, people sometimes confuse standing on the side of truth with wanting to be right. Believing that one must be right is grounded in unhelpful thinking—a topic I will be covering later in this book.

Chapter 3--Bad Arguments of Muslims and Christians

It's surprising how many people don't find it necessary to understand things in order to argue about them. Anonymous

In this short chapter I want to offer some typical bad arguments made by Muslims at the level of logos. I describe them not so much in the hope that Christians will use them "against" Muslims but so that Christians can identify these logical mistakes and not be taken in by them. Knowing and understanding these logical errors can be instructive and deepen one's own faith. For this reason, I think it is a good idea that those who attend church, beginning in junior high school should probably be introduced to these topics and thereby grasp more fully why they believe what they believe and the typical arguments offered against their faith.

Muslims: A Convoluted Straw Man Argument

A straw man argument is a form of informal logical fallacy, or error in argument, that is made when one advances a critique of an argument but instead of taking on the argument as it really is, the individual oversimplifies the argument or distorts it and then tries to point out the errors in the distorted argument (the distorted argument is a straw man or false argument because no one really holds that argument).

This kind of fallacy is frequently offered by Muslims. For example, two Muslims who have committed this fallacy in their critique of the Christian position that Jesus is God are Jamal Badawi and H. M. Baagil. You can find their arguments on the internet.

Badawi in an online article entitled, "Jesus in the Quran and Bible" advances reasons why the Christian claim that Jesus is divine because he performs a series of miracles and only someone who could perform such miracles is divine. The list of miracles offered by Badawi, that he thinks are advanced by Christians, is as follows:

+Jesus was born without a father
+Jesus fed the multitudes
+Jesus walked on water
+Jesus healed the lepers and the blind
+Jesus brought the dead to life
+Jesus cast the devils
+Jesus rose from the dead
+Jesus ascended to heavens

Badawi's strategy is to show that someone other than Jesus also performed each of these miracles, and therefore, there is nothing special about Jesus. Thus he couldn't be divine. He directs Christians to look at biblical verses as support for his claim. The verses he offers for each miracle are as follows:

+Born without a father: Hebrews 7:3
+Fed the multitudes: II Kings 4:42-44
+Walked on water: "similar to Moses" Exodus 14:22
+Healed the lepers and blind: II Kings 5:14, 6:17, 20; Acts 3:7, 5:15-16
+Brought the dead to life: I Kings 17:22, II Kings 4:34, 13:21; Ezekiel 37:1-14
+Cast the devils: Matthew 7:22, 12:27, Luke 11:19
+Rose from the dead: Ezekiel 37:1-14
+Ascended to heavens: Genesis 5:24; Hebrews 11:5; II Kings 2:11-12

Badawi's argument fails because it is a straw man fallacy. No Christian argues that because Jesus was born without a father that Jesus was divine. Sure, perhaps there are people who were born without a father. Badawi seems to think that pointing out this possibility refutes the Christian claim. It doesn't. Why? Because no Christian who is the least bit logical would make such an argument. The strategy is the same throughout Badawi's attempted refutation.

What Christians claim is that all these miracles are performed by just one person and that all these miracles taken as a whole point to his divinity. To refute the Christian argument, Badawi would have to produce a person other than Jesus who has performed *all* these miracles. Of course, Christians do not believe that Jesus is divine simply because he performed a long series of miracles. There are other reasons, but on this point about miracles, Badawi misses the point and ends up committing a straw man fallacy.

Another person who commits a straw man fallacy is H. M. Baagil in his online booklet, "Christian-Muslim Dialogue." Baagil's argument against the evidence Christians produce to support the divinity of Jesus takes the following form:

+Christian evidence: Jesus is filled with the Holy Spirit
++Baagil's counterevidence: Barnabas was filled with the Holy Spirit
+Christian evidence: Jesus fed the 5,000
++Baagil's counterevidence: Elisha and Elijah miraculously fed large numbers of people with little food
+Christian evidence: Jesus could heal leprosy
++Baagil's counterevidence: Elisha healed Naaman the leper
+Christian evidence: Jesus could raise the dead
++Bagail's counterevidence: Elijah raised a child from the dead
+Christian evidence: Jesus walked on water
++Baagil's counterevidence: Moses parted the sea
+Christian evidence: Jesus cast out demons
++Baagil's counterevidence: Disciples cast out demons

Baagil's strategy is the same flawed strategy of Badawi.

Muslims: Bandwagon Arguments

For years some Muslims have argued that Islam is superior to Christianity and is the true faith because it is growing at a faster rate worldwide than is Christianity. It is an empirical claim that Islam is growing at a faster rate worldwide. Like all empirical claims, it is either true or false and whether it is true or false is discernible (Karl Popper would say that it is falsifiable) by simply checking the numbers for the rate of growth. However, it cannot be empirically determined whether Islam is true or superior even if it is growing faster than Christianity. "That Islam is superior because it is growing faster than Christianity" is an argument, and for that argument to be valid there has to be a proper relationship between the claim and the supporting reasons. The structure of the argument is as follows:

+**Claim:** Islam is true and superior to Christianity
++**Supporting reason:** Islam is growing faster worldwide than Christianity.
+++**Warrant:** If a religion is growing faster worldwide than another faith, the one growing faster is superior and the true faith.

In logic the supporting reason must be both relevant and adequate/sufficient to support the claim fully. If the supporting reasons fail on either criterion, there is said to be a material fallacy present. If the supporting reason isn't relevant to the claim, it is called a material fallacy of relevance. If the supporting reason isn't adequate to fully support the claim, then it is said to be a material fallacy of insufficient evidence.

The argument under consideration is an example of a material fallacy of relevance, specifically what is often called the bandwagon fallacy. The truth or superiority of a religion can't be established by looking at the rate of growth. There are many reasons why a religion could grow at a faster rate other than being the true or superior faith. Some such reasons might be as follows:

+The religion is simpler to understand than another faith. Some truths are difficult to grasp.
+More people may embrace a faith because it is easy to follow. Living out the truth may simply not be easy to do.
+The religion is simply a fad, just as Transcendental Meditation was 30-40 years ago.

+The faith is doing a better job marketing itself than another faith.
+The faith is novel and people may be curious about it

Currently the belief system that is growing at the fastest rate worldwide is atheism. Surely believers in God wouldn't want to develop an argument that atheism is the true or superior faith. The rate of growth does not establish the truthfulness or superiority of a faith.

Another example of a material fallacy of relevance is the argument that Islam is superior to Christianity and is the true faith because it is a complete way of life. This is a longstanding argument offered by many conservative Muslims in the West. They claim that Islam includes a comprehensive theory of economics, criminal justice principles, regulations for marriage, principles of personal morality, and even for practical matters such as eating, drinking, dressing, and interpersonal relations. The warrant is clear: if a religion sets forth a complete way of life, it is the true or superior faith. What is wrong with this logic?
+One could duplicate Islam and then add still other rules of life based on recent findings in psychology, sociology, and medicine. Then according to the logic of these Muslims, the newly formed "faith" would be superior to Islam.
+One can develop a comprehensive way of life grounded in delusions or hallucinations. It would be a complete way of life, but the completeness would not be grounded in truth or reality.

One of the reasons I like Christianity is that it permits its adherents to use the mind given to them by God and thereby grow in faith and maturity. In the book of Job, God twice says to Job, "Gird your loins and be a man. I ask the questions, and you come up with the answers." God trusts us to make adequate decisions about life without giving us a detailed blueprint for life covering every possible life situation. Why would God do this? I don't claim to know why, but perhaps it is a consequence of the fact that we are created in the image of God with all the rights and duties of that status, including using reason to discern the right and good way of life.

31

Christians: Bad Arguments

The moon god argument: I have heard Christians and non-Christians alike argue against the validity of Islam by claiming that in pre-Islamic Arabia, Allah was a moon god. There are some good arguments grounded in archeological evidence substantiating that pre-Islamic Arabs used the word 'Allah' and that the word referred to a moon god. So what! Even if there was historical development in the descriptions of the nature of Allah such that Muhammad, and others, gradually came to reject Allah as a moon god and to conceptualize Allah as a transcendent God not attached to heavenly objects, that does not prove that Allah is not the true God. The point is that no contemporary Muslim believes in a moon god, so even if there has been development in the Arab understanding of God, Muslims no longer believe in a moon God—and they haven't for centuries. Perhaps Christians could claim that development in the conceptualization of the nature of Allah argues against the Muslim belief that the Muslim understanding of Allah is the same as that understood by early Jews and Christians who came before Islam and that Islam is a confirmation of those conceptions of God. Ok, but to say to current day Muslims that their conception of Allah grew out of a false God, does nothing but alienate Muslims. What a strange mission strategy--insult Muslims into the Kingdom.

The Deuteronomy 18:18 approach: The verse reads,

"I will raise up for them a prophet like you from among their brethren; and I will put my words in his mouth, and he shall speak to them all that I command him."

Both Muslims and Christians claim this verse as relevant to their prophet. Christians read the verse as pointing to Jesus and Muslims read it as pointing to Muhammad. Of course, as a Christian, I see the verse as more clearly pointing to Jesus, but Muslims see it quite differently. Therefore adherents of both faiths try to outdo the other by creating a longer list of relevant ways in which the verse points to their prophet over the other's prophet. The result is that the arguments go nowhere. Why is this the case? It is because of the inherent ambiguity of analogies. I have already covered the problem with analogies. Moses is like a lot of people in many different ways. Moses is also not like a lot of people in many different ways. There are relevant similarities between Moses and Jesus, but they are not identical, so there are also many relevant dissimilarities between the two. Even Christians should acknowledge this since Jesus is divine, but Moses isn't. There are relevant similarities between Moses and Muhammad, but they are certainly not identical, so there are also many relevant dissimilarities between the two. Because there is no identity relationship between the two, the other faith can always point out the dissimilarities between the other's prophet and Moses and highlight the relevant similarities between Moses and their prophet. Faith permits us to see the power of the relevant similarities, but without the faith, one sees differently. This should not be a surprise to Christians because in II Corinthians 5:16-17 we read,

"From now on, therefore, we regard no one from a human point of view; even though we once knew Christ from a human point of view, we know him no longer in that way. So if anyone is in Christ, there is a new creation; everything old has passed away; see, everything has become new."

Asking a Muslim to view this verse from a new point of view as if he or she were a Christian is a futile task.

Chapter 4--Muslim Misunderstandings about the Bible

Muslims often believe in the complete integrity of the Qur'an in its current form, which means it contains no errors in any form. Moreover, they often claim that it has never been subject to any form of corruption and the Qur'an today is in its original revealed form as compiled during the caliphate of Uthman. The assumption is that for a book to come from God or to be truly inspired by God it must be completely free from any problems whatsoever. Many Christians hold the same view about the Bible. Thus many Muslims try to show the textual and logical integrity of the Qur'an and the Bible's lack of such integrity. Likewise, some Christians try to show the textual and logical integrity of the Bible and the Qur'an's lack of such. I am not a fan of this approach because it focuses on the wrong issues and often just devolves into defensiveness and an "I match you and raise you" form of debate that never seems to get to the issue of a live relationship with Jesus. That said, let me focus on some misunderstandings many Muslims may have about the Bible so you have idea what might be going on in the Muslim's head. I never debate these points with Muslims, but when they present, I simply try to gently share the role of the Bible in my life and its primary goal for me, namely, to witness to God's faithfulness toward all of us throughout history, especially as evidenced in the life and person of Jesus and how we humans can enter into a beautiful saving relationship with God through Jesus.

+**Errors in the Bible?** John Gilchrist (1999) in a traditional work of apologetics touches on this issue with great integrity but in a way many evangelicals would criticize. Gilchrist states that there are some errors in the Bible and that these largely numerical errors are simply copy errors (36). For example 2 Kings 24:8 says that Jehoiachin was eight years old when he became king and 2 Chronicles 36:9 says that he was eighteen. From Gilchrist's perspective, it is obvious that a single Hebrew letter was omitted in copying the text. Gilchrist discusses four such copy errors.

Some Christians flatly deny the presence of even minor copy errors in the Bible. While one could might deny copy errors in the Bible, one could argue from the stance of "what if, hypothetically, the Bible were to contain some minor copy errors." One then hypothetically admits the issue and then points out that not one of these purported errors touches on the integrity of the message of the Bible. Whether Jehoichin was eight or eighteen in no way erases the salvation story, the need of humans for redemption, and the way to be in right relationship with God.

Continuing in this hypothetical vein, even if purportedly there are some minor copy errors in the Bible, does it mean that the Bible is worthless? For a guy who is not terribly fond of analogical arguments, let me offer a couple. If after a long search I find the "perfect" car, buy it, and then I find a very small, almost imperceptible scratch on it, what should I do? I suppose I could irrationally disturb myself and end up uttering, "It is totally ruined; I have to take it back immediately." The car still does an exemplary job doing what the primary purpose of a car is—move me from point A to point B safely, comfortably, and without using too much gas. It also looks pretty cool to someone who doesn't freak out over the minor scratch. Clearly, my emotional reaction would be exaggerated and misses the purpose of having a car and that it still looks pretty good. To declare that the Bible is worthless if it contains copy errors is to be histrionic and irrational.

Let me offer another analogy. My father died seven years ago and shortly after his death, I received a number of pictures of him. One is my all-time favorite—a picture of dad when he was about three years old. He was wearing bibbed overalls and was standing on an old beat up car. He was staring right into the camera with just a touch of a smile on his face. It was a smile I knew well. That picture captured a truth about my dad in a way no other picture ever has. I love the picture, but in reality it is grainy, faded, and has a long white streak running along the bottom third of the picture. It is a damaged picture, but the damage does not detract from the truth of the picture. But then again, I look at the picture out of love for my dad wanting to experience something of him despite the fact that he is gone. Others might just see the damaged picture. If I were to focus on the obvious defects in the picture rather than on the truth of the entire picture, I would never feel deeply about a memory of experiencing the soul of my father. I gladly accept the scratches to remember my dad again and the blessing I experienced through him during my life with him. The picture is in a prominent place within my office.

It is interesting that Maurice Bucaille (1977) had the intellectual integrity to admit that some of the oldest existing manuscripts of the Qur'an (attributed to the caliph Uthman, the third caliph after the death of Muhammad) that exist in Tashkent and Istanbul contain such errors. Similarly, ancient copies of the Qur'an as found in Paris and elsewhere in Europe contain problems. Bucaille writes,

"The numerous ancient texts that are known to be in existence all agree except for very minor variations which do not change the general meaning of the text at all" (p. 131).

Both Gilchrist and Bucaille seem to agree that the emphasis should be on more substantial issues in those texts without the distraction of comparing numbers of purported copy errors. At this point some Christians may be appalled that I am admitting copy errors in the Bible. I am not. I am just being myphilosopher self and saying that even if hypothetically the Bible did contain some copy errors, that in no way touches on any essential issue within the Bible. To pretend that it does is a mere diversionary tactic. I am not going to waste my time looking for copy errors in the Qur'an either. Why not? I am about substance, not about the fact that the ancients lacked copy machines. I have deep concerns about some of the content of the Qur'an as interpreted by some Muslims. However, even that is not my major concern. I do not want to spend my time talking about the Qur'an or even about whether the Bible has been preserved perfectly. My interest is in the content of the Bible on which all Christians agree—Jesus. I want to share Jesus, not count printing errors or anything else that detracts from the centrality of Jesus to our faith and the need all of us have for Him.

+Why Four Gospels? Some Muslims are confused by the presence of four Gospels in the Bible and that the authors are believed to be Matthew, Mark, Luke, and John. As a Christian I don't see the problem. For me, the greater number of Gospels, the better. Why is it that when there is an automobile accident it is better to have a number of witnesses than simply one witness? Sure each witness may focus on a different aspect of the accident and each may have stories that differ in details, but in these stories we can be more certain of the reality and even the details of the event. Details get filled in that might be missed if there was only one witness. Husserl, the famous father of phenomenology said that truth is the unity in the multiplicity of perspectives. The fewer the number of accounts of biblical or Qur'anic events, the less certainty we have about the nature and aspects of the event. Unfortunately, many of the Qur'anic manuscripts were burned so we no longer have access to potential multiple additional details. There are thousands of Bible manuscripts that help us approach near certainty about the events in the Bible.

A confusion of some Muslims is about the nature of the Injil (the Gospels). Many believe that it was Allah-inspired, perhaps through the Angel Gabriel, and that the message of the Injil was received by Jesus in book form. So, supposedly Jesus received a message that could have been put in a single book and carried around with him. For those Muslims, if that is true, then it is confusing how there could be four Gospels. Their assumption about the nature of revelation makes it difficult for them to see the advantage of multiple Gospels.

Given the Muslim assumption about revelation, we can see why many would be confused about the presence in the New Testament of so many books written by Paul and others. They are looking for a book written by God and received by Jesus. No such book ever existed.

Some Muslims are able to see that in Christianity there is what might be taken to be an interesting parallel with Islam. For many Muslims the two major sources of authority are the Qur'an and hadith. They take the Qur'an to be the literal words of Allah revealed to Muhammad through the Angel Gabriel over a period of twenty three years. The hadith are purportedly accounts of what Muhammad said or descriptions of what he did in particular circumstances. There are two types of hadith: one type is the words of Muhammad or eyewitnesses of Muhammad and the other are directly inspired by Allah but written in the words of Muhammad. Both types of hadith have two parts: the matn and the isnad. The matn is the content and the isnad is the list of individuals who transmitted the hadith purportedly all the way back to Muhammad, or an eyewitness. Muslims are very serious in their desire to be meticulous about rightly attributing words and actions to Muhammad so they have historically developed a science of isnad to maximize the possibility of, but never actually guaranteeing, the accuracy of the matn. One might consider Matthew, Mark, Luke, John, Paul, Peter, and others as part of an isnad that traces the content of the New Testament back to Jesus. The New Testament content goes a bit further with these inspired authors helping the reader/hearer grasp the significance of the life, words, and person of Jesus for the believing community.

So for Christians, the New Testament is not a book revealed by the Angel Gabriel to Jesus, but a collection of various accounts of Jesus by eyewitnesses and those who were linked to these eyewitnesses. The important issue isn't ultimately the number of books, but the inspired nature of those books.

+**Versions of the Bible**. Again, this is an issue that confuses many Muslims. It is true that there are multiple translations of the Bible into hundreds of languages, but informed Christians realize that these translations are not without error and each translation involves an interpretation of the meaning of the oldest manuscripts in the original language. Actually, I like the way Muslims deal with this issue with respect to the Qur'an. They

38

often insist that the Qur'an is the original revelation in the original language, Arabic. Any other "version" of the Qur'an is merely a translation of the perceived meaning of the original revelation and is not to be confused with the true Qur'an. That is exactly what we Christians should say about the Bible. The inerrancy is in the original revelation, not in the NIV, King James, Oxford Annotated Bible, etc. Version is merely translation.

Now, there is a difference in the number of books in the Roman Catholic and Protestant Bibles. The difference is that the Roman Catholic Bible contains seven more books in it that are intertestamental in nature, or roughly cover the history between the Old Testament and the New Testament. However, as it was stated in the discussion about the copy errors in the Bible, namely, that the problems do not touch on essentials of the faith for practicing Christians of any type, the same can be said about the differences between the Protestant and Roman Catholic versions of the Bible. What is contained in the seven disputed books neither adds to nor subtracts from the basic message of the Christian faith, viz., humans are in need of redemption, we are in a broken relationship with God, Jesus and his life and work can repair that relationship, and if one allows that to happen, there are eternal and temporal consequences.

Most spiritually mature practicing Christians move beyond mere denominationalism or a particular translation of the Bible to emphasize a relationship with God celebrated in a community of believers. We know that whatever flavor Christian someone is or whatever name is on the church, it is the same Holy Spirit moving through us, the same God who is being worshipped, and the same Jesus who gave us the possibility for eternal meaning, purpose, and joy. The rest is "tchotchke."

+Original sin. This concept or reality deeply divides Christians and Muslims. It is on this topic that people start pulling jargon out of their theological closets, a lot like Job's friends when they get into their unhelpful responses to Job's pain. Let's go back to basics. Most Christians believe that there was a time when immediately after the creation of humans by God that we were in a state of original purity and bliss. We had free will, but we had not exercised it in an immature rebellious way. Most Muslims believe the same. When the Qur'an reads that we humans were created in the best form, we Christians are in agreement, by and large, at least about the original humans. Both also agree that at some point humans exercised their free will in a rebellious way with seriously negative consequences. It is at this point we get bogged down in many ways—some trivial, and some not so trivial. Many Christians describe the consequences as a fall from grace marked by a radical ontological change in humans such that our original predisposition to exercise our will in obedience to God became radically corrupted such that we humans now have a pervasive disposition to rebel against God in thought, word, and deed. Often we call this, The Fall.

Most Muslims do not believe that there was a major negative ontological change in humans that has continued to persist over time. In fact, many Muslims believe that humans are still in the best form—at least at birth. However, these same Muslims often embrace the belief that there is a pervasive tendency within humans to forget Allah, resulting in negative consequences for those humans. That is part of the reason behind praying five times per day as a means of remembering Allah. The pervasiveness of the tendency to forget Allah necessitates not only the five daily prayers but four other pillars of actions required of Muslims and a host of ways to act in the ways that Muhammad did as a way to remember Allah. For example, in the hadith we learn that when Muhammad broke his fast he ate an odd number of dates, when he went to the bathroom he entered on his left foot and exited on his right foot, he didn't breath into a glass of water when he was drinking, he would not stand when he went to the bathroom, he would wear perfume to the mosque, he would use a miswak (part of a small specific kind of tree branch) to clean his teeth before prayer, he handed people items with his right hand rather than his left hand, etc. There are many more actions that are described and many observant Muslims earnestly want to copy them in their lives as a way to glorify Allah and to remember Allah in all their actions throughout the day.

As a philosopher, I wrestle with what a Muslim does not grasp about "The Fall". If we are truly created in the best form, not just "a very good form" or "an adequate form", then what aspect of our ontology, our being, is disrupted such that the human forgetfulness of Allah would arise? Whatever aspect of our being gave rise to this forgetfulness could not have been created in the best form or at least certainly that form isn't pervasive in our present being. If that weakness is within us, how can we be said to be in the best form? A more accurate account might be to say that much within humans is good but that there is a confused, or broken, or perverse part within us and that try as we might to do the good, we end up making a mess of things pretty regularly. Look at the world, including Muslim populated countries. There is goodness, but there is also a whole lot of messiness.

I don't really care whether you call this deep and pervasive negative part of the self that causes such hurt and pain within the world, original sin, the consequences of The Fall, or a form of radical forgetfulness within us that has us do evil. Call it what you want, but the evil comes from us, even when we don't want to do evil. There is a major problem in our being and in the world, and all our efforts to overcome this problem through law, cultural reform, building more churches and mosques, practicing meditation, taking anger management classes, etc., have not corrected the problem. Why? Because we are the problem, not the origin of a solution to the problem.

In the history of Islam there were Muslims who were upset with how the caliphs after the rightly guided caliphs, the leaders of the Islamic world deviated drastically from the ideal life purportedly set forth by Muhammad. One such group was the Sufis, or Muslim mystics, who tried to urge Muslims to move beyond the mere externals of the faith as found in Islamic law and customs to move toward a purification of the heart. They saw that the problem was in the human heart and that it needed to be healed and transformed. But even the rise of Sufism was not able

41

to overcome or eliminate the pervasive tendency in Muslims to do evil. This is not just a Muslim problem; it is a Christian problem, and a human problem. Historians describe two Great Awakenings of faith that took place in the United States and thousands of churches have held revivals, but we in the United States, including the Christians, are a mess and we cause all kinds of evil in the world.

Call it what you will, the evidence points to the fact that there is a serious problem in the human heart. It is universal and people around the world are dying, starving, murdering, committing suicide, giving up hope, and failing to love—all because of the serious problem in the human heart. Whatever you call it, it needs to be healed...and it can be...if Christians will share how to be healed. Let that be our focus.

+**Muhammad in the Bible**. Many Muslims believe the Qur'an gives a veiled prophecy of someone who was to come after Jesus who would be called Ahmad. Some contemporary Muslim scholars claim that Ahmad (or Muhammad) is almost a translation of the Greek word, periclytos. They say that in John 14:16, 15:26, and 16:7 the word "comforter" is a translation of the Greek word, paracletos. They contend that paracletos is a corrupt reading for periclytos. Unfortunately for the Muslim, in Greek, unlike Arabic, the vowels are written into the text. To change periclytos to paracletos would require alteration of three written letters, so it couldn't even have been a copy error, or a copy error would be highly unlikely. Moreover, not one of the ancient manuscripts of John includes the word periclytos. Also, while the word periclytos was used frequently by Homer in the Odyssey and Iliad, not once is it used in the koine Greek of the New Testament or the Septuagint. Thus, this is just confirmatory bias on the part of these Muslims. It is a form of emotional reasons, namely, "because something seems reasonable, it must exist." Another way to state the problem more philosophically is "what is logical may not be ontological." What seems to be logical to us may not actually be the reality. That is why science employs multiple methods of acquiring and evaluating data rather than having scientists merely sit in a room and think.

Some Muslims even find references to Muhammad in the Old Testament. For example, read Psalm 84 and see whether you can find a reference to Muhammad. Do that before you read any further in this book. If you failed to see the reference to Muhammad, don't beat yourself up. To their eyes the reference is in verses 5-6. They argue that the Valley of Baca is actually Mecca. Apparently, at the time of Muhammad, southern Arabic interchanged "b" and "m" so to these Muslims scholars it seems reasonable for the reference to be to Mecca. Christian and Jewish scholars note that in the original Hebrew, the phrase for Valley of Baca is *emeg ha-Baka*, which has been translated as the Valley of the Balsam Tree or Valley of the Weeper. In the Oxford Annotated Bible one finds a footnote indicating that Baca was some unknown desolate place through which the pilgrims must go. Apparently, in Jewish tradition Psalm 84 is characterized as a psalm of pilgrimage. While the Muslim reading of this psalm has face validity, it is certainly bizarre for a single psalm to make a reference to Mecca. It would be interesting to read these Muslim scholars and how they interpret the link between Mecca and Zion in the psalm My hope is that Muslims would read verse 2, "My soul longs, yea, faints for the courts of the Lord; my heart and flesh sing for joy to the living God." Their hearts long for the Lord, the living God. When Muslims want me to read this psalm and what they think is a reference to Mecca, I always go to verse 2 and talk about that reality. I also frequently get around to a related issue addressed by Ismail al-Faruqi (1986). In response to a question posed by Lamin Sanneh, then at the University of Legon, Ghana, Faruqi said, "You spoke of god willing and wanting to reveal Himself to man. God does not reveal Himself. He does not reveal Himself to anyone in any way. God reveals only his will" (p. 17). So our soul, heart, and flesh long for and sing for joy to the living god, but according to Faruqi, all a Muslim can hope for is the will of God, which is to be found in Islamic law. We humans do not long for will; we can only submit to a will. However, our deep longing is for the reality of God. That is what Muslims really want and we can help them find the true object of that longing. Gilson, the famous Roman Catholic theologian and philosopher, allegedly said, "Why settle for the shadow of God when you can have the reality?"

Chapter 5--Bad Science in Defense of Islam

Science is one of the greatest human achievements with many major positive influences on the quality of human life. It is not a mystery why Muslims often appeal to science in their attempt to persuade non-Muslims, and perhaps themselves, of the validity of the Qur'an and the call of Muhammad. Muhammad Haykal (1976) says,

The reader may be surprised by our emphasis on the similarity of Muhammad's teachings to the methods of modern science. The scientific method demands that were one to undertake an investigation, he should suspend his personal views, beliefs, and doctrines. Thus scientific method is the highest human achievement in the cause of free thought. And yet this very method is none other than that of Muhammad, the very foundation of his cause (p. 93).

These above lines followed a very short presentation of the initial call of Muhammad as prophet. The appeal to science was also invoked by Haykal to support the possibility of the Isra and Miraj, and the "miracle" of the cave of thauwr (an episode that was omitted in Ibn Hisham's biography of Muhammad).

The appeal to science in da'wah (invitation to non-Muslims to embrace Islam) is seen most clearly in The Bible, the Qur'an and Science by Maurice Bucaille. It and numerous posts on Youtube demonstrate how many contemporary Muslims attempt to show not only how the content of the Qur'an and hadith are consistent with scientific "facts" but also predated scientific findings that were made centuries after the compilation of the Qur'an. There are two basic flaws common to all such attempts:
+Specificity is read into general statements (i.e., several statements are viewed as saying more than they actually say)
+Statements are read as prophecy when it is more reasonable for them to be read as revealing the science pre-dating Islam or

contemporary with Islam. The pre-scientific statements are then anachronistically read as scientific.

I am not going to belabor these points but will simply give some illustrations of these logical errors so you will know them when you hear them. However, when you hear Muslims repeat these logical errors, listen for the desire beneath the error. These Muslims are serious about their faith, they love and respect the message of the Qur'an, and they want its message to be consistent with the scientific world view they have also embraced. Be respectful rather than simply attack their logical errors. Remember that your goal is not to destroy someone's faith (or at least I hope that is the case), but to call them to the truth.

Seven Heavens? Literal or Symbolic?

Bucaille notes that in the Qur'an the number seven "refers to the heavens themselves" (140). He notes that Qur'anic commentators are in agreement that the number is not meant to be taken literally but is symbolic or refers to plurality. He offers no argument to justify that on this point the Qur'an is to be taken symbolically. It is important for such a justification to be offered since on other Qur'anic passages commentators often interpret them quite literally when if anything is to be taken symbolically it would be these passages. For example, in the online Salafiyyah book, The General Prescripts of Belief in the Qur'an and Sunnah, we read,

Allah the Most High speaks to his slaves as He wishes. He descends and comes closer to His slaves as He wills. He has a face, a hand a leg and a foot. Yet none of the attributes of His essence resembles those of human beings.

As a philosopher, I have no idea what this passage really means. Either it is symbolic, which I can grasp; or is analogical, in which case the meaning isn't clear at all and more akin to poetry; or it is literal, which would simply be crass anthropomorphism. However we are to take it, there must be a

46

principle, or principles, by which we can determine how we are to interpret the passage or simply assume that we are to accept it at face value without interpreting it at all. Then the emphasis would be on an act of the will on our part rather than an act of reason. I don't care which, but it would be helpful to know the principle or principles that we are to use to interpret the Qur'an.

The issue of Qur'anic interpretation aside, there may still be another reason why the number seven is used to refer to the heavens. [For those of you interested in reading some of these Qur'anic verses mentioning the seven heavens see: 2:29, 23:17, 67:3, 71:15-16, 78:12]. This other reason is grounded in history and is more probable than an arbitrary declaration that the verse is symbolic. There were pre-Islamic apocryphal writings that could easily have been known to pre-Islamic Arabs. While no ancient manuscripts of the Torah or New Testament refer to the seven heavens and so were never a part of those texts, they do appear in some other sources with religious significance. Johnson notes that Charles has written that the notion of the seven heavens was present in an apocryphal book entitled, The Book of the Secrets of Enoch (218). References were also in the Jewish midrash. For example in the Midrash ha-Ne'elam it reads,

Rabbi Johannan said, This Rakia' (heaven) that was created on the second day (of creation) is the uppermost one...All the other heavens were made out of this one...Scriptures call it both Rakia' and Shamayim (Gen. 1:8) because Shamayim was made of Rakia'. And that heaven bore all the other heavens which came out of it. (Johnson, 218-19)

Katsh quotes R. Me'ir, Resh Lakish, R. Eleazar, and R. Eliezer all as saying there are seven heavens. The Midrash also states that the wicked are deluded when they believe "that God does not see when they sin because He is separated from them by seven heavens...but God...sees everybody and everything." (Johnson, 219)

These statements in early Jewish sources are quite similar to what we see in the Qur'an, such as the following passage,

It is He who created for you all that is in the earth, then He made for the heavens and fashioned them seven heavens; and He knows all things. (2:27)

I suppose Muslims could try to use the fact of the absence of these references in the Bible as proof that the Bible has been corrupted. But what would be the motivation to remove all references to the seven heavens? It seems trivial and utterly irrational. If the ancient manuscripts mentioned seven heavens, no theological point would be gained or lost by removing these references. A more likely explanation is that the worldview in which Muhammad existed included this cosmology which was present at the time and had extra biblical origins. This is a more plausible explanation that does not have to appeal to conspiracy theories. The reality is that the Qur'an is a book that was created at a time when surrounding cultures believed in a cosmology that included seven heavens and this cosmology was incorporated into the Qur'an. This does not detract from the religious significance of the Qur'an and it solves the problem in part of what to take literally and what to take symbolically and what to take as reflective of cultural elements prior to and contemporaneous to the creation and compilation of the Qur'an. It also helps those of us who are Christians to interpret Paul's reference to the third heaven in II Corinthians 12:2-4. Rather than making a scientific point, Paul was most likely appealing to the levels of heavens in the rabbinic literature of the time.

What is interesting for me is not these points, but that some contemporary conservative Muslims whose world view is shaped by modern science for which the notion of seven heavens would not correspond to anything found in science, use contemporary science as a hermeneutical tool to interpret the Qur'an and thus see such verses as symbolic. So what determines how a verse is to be interpreted? I do not fault Muslims, and they can develop the hermeneutical principles that work for them. It is, however, something that they should address for this aspect of their faith to be reasonable. This goes to something asserted by Ismail al-Faruqi, one of the founders of the Muslim Student Association, the Islamic Society of North America, and the International Institute of Islamic Thought. He allegedly said that Islam has no problem with hermeneutics because of the preservation of Arabic lexicography and syntax (Johnson, 252). Clearly, Muslims do need to grapple with hermeneutics if they are to engage in dialogue with informed Christians who will ask questions of hermeneutics. This point was recognized by more modernist Muslims such as Fazlur Rahman and Mahmud Abu Rayyah. While it may be true that linguistic purity may make exegesis less problematical, the hermeneutical task of interpreting the meaning of the text remains.

These issues become critical in the next case in which many contemporary conservative Muslims appeal to demonstrate the scientific "miracles" within the Qur'an, i.e., human reproduction as described by the Qur'an. Bucaille spends a good amount of time in his book, The Bible, the Qur'an and Science on the issue of human reproduction. It is a simple argument. He seems to be claiming that in numerous Qur'anic verses it is stated that humans were created from a small quantity of sperm. [Qur'an 16:4, 23:13, 75:37]. The Qur'an apparently also says, according to Bucaille that humans were created from a "despised liquid" [Qur'an 32:8, 77:20]. If we just focus on these two attempts to demonstrate the scientific miracles within the Qur'an, there are already at least three apparent problems:
+The verses presuppose that it is the sperm that creates a human. Of course, these verses seem to embed a male bias that was common among ancient writers, such as Aristotle and even Aquinas, namely, it was the male that creates a human and that the woman is simply a passive receptacle.
+The only reason that sperm would be called a despised liquid would be if one presupposed either its intrinsic or acquired uncleanness. Bucaille says that it is because sperm travels

49

through the penis, which is used for urination, that sperm is despised. This reveals more about what Muslims at the time of Muhammad thought about cleanliness. In many forms of Islamic law, urination or ejaculation renders one ritually impure, necessitating a ritual wash before prayers can be offered to Allah.

Actually, a more basic problem is the basic strategy in dealing with these pre-scientific verses. A very general Qur'anic text is interpreted as revealing a very specific scientific fact and then creative exegesis takes place to read the pre-scientific bias as somehow revealing a contemporary scientific finding. The contemporary scientific "meaning" is then read into the pre-scientific Qur'anic texts. The human mind is amazing and can see things that aren't really there. Consider the pictures often found in introductory psychology textbooks to introduce Gestalt psychology. An incomplete picture is shown to an individual and the individual sees either a rabbit or a chalice, or an old woman or young woman. The human mind is not a passive receptor of reality but is actively engaged in creating pictures or interpretations of reality. There is a phenomenon called confirmatory bias, which is a tendency for people to favor information that confirms their beliefs. It often happens with issues that are emotionally charged or touch issues that are very entrenched in one's belief system.

Psychological experiments over the past fifty years demonstrate that people have a tendency to test their ideas in a very one-sided way such that they focus exclusively on one way to interpret the data and ignore other interpretations. Of course, this can lead to very biased conclusions. We end up seeing what we wish to be present more than that which is truly present. In the case of seeing modern scientific facts in the Qur'anic pre-scientific descriptions of human reproduction, much rides on seeing it as a scientific miracle. The cost of actually seeing it in its ancient historical light is huge, and that cost makes neutral exploration and explanation impossible or improbable.

I do not think it is horrible that Muslims interpret the Qur'an as prophesying scientific fact. I think they are wrong, but

50

their activity shows their love of the Qur'an and the seriousness with which they engage the book they love. I do not find it as important to attack those very human psychological dynamics as it is to understand them and help them see the world and faith in a broader way that helps them move toward the truth without defensively clinging to bias that limits them in very important ways. This should be done in a loving way, not a triumphant arrogant way.

Chapter 6--Models for Missions to Muslims

Remember that all models are wrong; the practical question is how wrong do they have to be to not be useful. –George Edward Pelham Box

While I am not big on models for missions, I want to cover the main models to introduce my non-model model. In this chapter I am going to rely very heavily on the work of Mark Terry and John Travis who wrote some excellent articles in the late 1990s. Terry (1996) has described what he describes as five major models for reaching Muslims:

+Confrontational
+Traditional Evangelical
+Institutional
+Dialogical
+Contextualization

Travis goes into more depth on the contextualization spectrum in an accessible way.

Confrontational Model: This is pretty easy to characterize. It is an attempt to win Muslims through oral debate and literature that is debate oriented. The strategy tends to be to show the deficiencies in Islam and the ways in which Christianity is superior, or right. There is a spectrum of approaches to debate within this model from highly academic literature to "down and dirty" emotionally loaded verbal fisticuffs. It can be relational in nature and proponents often justify the approach by saying that it is a culturally relevant form of interaction with many Muslims.

Alford (2008) has written about Jay Smith, one of the proponents of this approach and one who trains Christians to engage in in this approach with Muslims. Apparently Jay notes the following about his model:

+"Passionate presentation is one key to reaching Muslims"
+The approach is to defend historic, orthodox Christianity; answer untruths that Islam proclaims about the Bible, Jesus, and Christians; hold Islam itself accountable for the actions of its followers
+"We have to start taking Christ back to his Mediterranean roots." "True love confronts friends when they go wrong. Paul certainly argued. Jesus certainly argued. That the kind of love Muslims need to hear?'
+"Propositional truth confronts. If there's not a reaction, we're not preaching the gospel."
+"The gospel by definition is confrontational. I absolutely want to stop Islam because Islam is stopping these people."
+"The Qur'an has huge errors in it, enormous errors. My goal is to eradicate the whole edifice of Islam so that [Muslims] can then look for the alternative."

  With these beliefs, Jay Smith forcefully engages hundreds of Muslims who are gathered to debate at the famous Speakers Corner in Hyde Park in London. This approach is not without its proponents who agree with Jay, but also not without Christians who have reservations about the approach. For example, some say that while the model might work in Western countries, it probably would not be effective in Muslim populated countries. Others note that attacking the Qur'an is probably not as effective as portraying the Bible in a good light. Some suggest that it might be helpful to the church in keeping nominal Christians from being swayed by the arguments of Muslims. Terry notes that a strength of the approach is that it does attract a few intellectual Muslims to Christianity. This strength should be weighed against the model's potential weaknesses, namely, it is not very successful in terms of numbers of Muslims exposed to the approach coming to the Lord and it may increase antipathy toward Christians,
  Traditional Evangelical Model/Friendship Model. Over the past fifteen years of teaching Muslim studies courses to graduate students at a Christian university, I have found that most

of them embrace this model. Conceptually it is a simple model. Christians witness to Muslim individuals and small groups with an emphasis on the message of repentance, submission to Jesus, and involvement in the church. In some forms it is very church centered. Those who subscribe to this model spend time learning about the culture of the Muslim and in ways to show friendship in forms that Muslims would experience as friendship. Those who like this model say that it is consistent with scripture and that even if not highly efficient may actually sow seeds that may sprout later. The criticism of the model is that the approach isn't very successful in terms of numbers of converts and that by befriending Muslims, Christians may make their Muslim friends a target for social ostracism. Later I will cover the approach of George Houssney's brand of friendship evangelism that has some advice for avoiding social ostracism. It is a simple model that churches can launch without a big budget and can often create good will between Muslims and Christians. Is it successful? Frankly, this needs to be studied in more depth.

Institutional Model: Roman Catholics have employed this model for many years. It involves showing love to Muslims by serving them through institutions such as schools and hospitals. For a long time, this was perhaps the only way to reach Muslims. It is also helpful to overcome instances of Muslim prejudice toward Christianity. On the downside, it is expensive and as Muslim cultures advance, Muslim governments develop their own such institutions. It is interesting that recently on the television show, 60 Minutes, there was coverage of the Gulen Movement of 130 charter schools created in the United States by Turkish businessmen hiring primarily Turkish teachers to help upgrade the performance of American students in math and science. The schools have a huge waiting list of potential students because of the success of these schools. It is an example of what the West has done in Muslims countries for many years. Just as some Americans are concerned that these schools are a way to spread Islam in the United States, some Muslims have been concerned about the use of schools and hospitals to spread Christianity in Muslim populated countries.

Dialogical Model. Terry has written that this model has tried to reconcile the rift between Muslims and Christians primarily through four means: learning to appreciate Muslim beliefs, developing friendships, learning how to witness to Muslims, and bringing them to salvation in Christ. Some Christians have argued that this is not a separate model, but simply a variant of the Friendship Model. This model focuses on developing a deep understanding of and appreciation for Muslims. Critics point out that at times it may overemphasize similarities and under-emphasize differences. These critics wonder what the motivation would be for Muslims to embrace Christianity if the similarities between the faiths are great and the differences are never spelled out. Many evangelical Christians believe that this model is primarily the model of more liberal Christians.

Contextualization. This is a complex model that takes many different forms. However, at base the approach is for Christians to become like Muslims externally so as to reduce the resistance of Muslims to accept the Gospel. Roughly, the strength of this model is that unlike some of the others, it does not conflate the Christian message with Western culture and cultural trappings. One criticism of the model is that it can, in its extreme forms, severely blur the distinction between Christianity and Islam, or more concretely, an individual's religious identity. Some question whether it is possible for someone to be a Muslim Christian or Christian Muslim. What would these identities mean in the mind, heart, and practice of the individual? If someone becomes a new being in Christ, how radical is this new being? To what degree does this new being involve a complete overhauling of religious practices? Does the form of practice carry with it an identity? Can two individuals exhibiting the same religious practice have totally different religious identities and religious intentionality? These are very deep and interesting questions---and as you may imagine are vigorously debated.

55

John Travis (1999) has broken down contextualization into six subtypes along a continuum, which are designated as C1-C6. Roughly, the greater the C-number, the greater the degree of contextualization, and the greater the degree of controversy among Christians. Before introducing the spectrum, please note that it is impossible not to contextualize the Christian message and practices to some degree. One must communicate in a language that is grasped by the Muslim and to do so is to contextualize. C1 is marked by very little contextualization in that it tends to bring Muslims into traditional churches populated by Christians who have cultures that are foreign to the local Muslims. The Christians use their "churchy" language in a foreign tongue that may not be fully grasped by the Muslim. In many ways this may involve inviting the Muslim to Western Christianity.

What is termed C2 is a step toward greater contextualization in that the language used within the church is the language of the local Muslims, although the vocabulary is distinctively Christian. The cultural forms are distinctively non-Muslim (are often Western). C3 is still a further step toward greater contextualization. The language used is the language of the local Muslims and the cultural forms are more "Muslim" or the forms of dress and music used by the local Muslims. The religious forms are, however, not Muslim. For example, the individuals would not observe the Muslim form of fast during Ramadan, recite the Qur'an, or go on hajj. In other words, the cultural forms that are embraced are those that are more religiously neutral.

Most Christians do not have objections to C1-3. However, as we reach C4, the objections increase markedly. In C4 we see Christ-centered communities that use the language of the local Muslims and also use what some would see as biblically permissible cultural and Islamic forms. For example, Muslims/Christians embracing this degree of contextualization might only eat halal food, might only dress in Islamically permissible forms of dress, might continue keeping the Ramadan fast, etc. The communities would be comprised primarily of Muslim background believers (MBBs) who to the surrounding

Muslim community would not be seen as Muslims despite the fact that they may identify themselves as followers of the Prophet Isa (Jesus). C5 is still more debated because these Jesus-centric communities of Messianic Muslims, or Muslims who have accepted Jesus as Lord, remain legally Muslims and practice in mosques. They may develop a Messianic mosque and meet regularly with fellow Messianic Muslims, but they may also worship with traditional Muslims. Many Christians wonder about the degree of identity confusion experienced by such believers. Are they creating a new religious form that is not fully Christian or fully Muslim? What are the necessary and sufficient conditions for someone to be a Muslim or a Christian? What is a person who mixes the necessary conditions? Could someone embrace the sufficient conditions for both faiths? What is going on in the mind and heart of such a believer?

Less controversial is C6, but even it is not fully noncontroversial. This is where, for fear of persecution, small secret or underground Jesus-centric communities are formed. These believers may identify themselves as Muslims but experience themselves as Christians in a clearer way than the C5 believers would. Some Christians argue that these underground believers should be bolder and more willing to accept whatever potential consequences there are as a result of their conversion. It is so easy for safe Western Christians to argue that underground believers should be willing to die for their faith when these Western Christians have only to lose time and gas money when they openly drive to and from church. A more appropriate response would be to empathize with these secret believers.

Two Examples

In the following section of this book I will cover two examples of approaches to reach Muslims that while marked by significant differences, emphasize reaching Muslims with love and respect. As you read them, try to identify them vis-à-vis the models I have just discussed. Let me give you a hint. The model or approach of Carl Medearis is clearly in the contextualization camp. I leave it to you to see where it is along the C1-C6 contextualization continuum. George Houssney tends not to embrace contextualization, so how would you characterize his approach? I have only met Carl once in Colorado at a gathering in which both of us spoke. I have known and interacted with George over several years. I have tried to be true to their texts and fairly describe their approaches without distortion.

Carl Medearis

Carl is not a traditional academic, but he is deeply practical, relational, loving, and seemingly comfortable with ambiguity—all great traits. He enjoys relating to Muslims and it shows. For example in Muslims, Christians and Jesus he writes,

Because Christians believe, as do Muslims, that there is only one God, we have an opportunity to enjoy much shared ground. Notice I said enjoy. I did not say exploit. It is very critical to keep in mind how sacred the faith of the Muslim is to him. Do not treat it with disregard (p. 48)

Carl says that when he starts talking to Muslims he tries to stay focused on Jesus, not the Qur'an or Muhammad or terrorism. He encourages Christians to move away from stereotypes about Muslims (he too tends toward a nominalist approach). Carl focuses on practical ways to interact with Muslims such as,
+**Have fun!** Don't think of evangelizing or strategies and end up being overly serious about interacting with Muslims. Have fun with them. Relate to them as people, not projects.
+**No agenda.** He says that our real agenda ought to be to do the good and serve people in the name of Jesus. The agenda is not to convert, fix Muslims, or save them. We can't do that anyway. So try loving them.
+**Be a-religious**. You are not the appointed attorney for the religion of Christianity, so don't be defensive, argumentative, or act like you know it all. Lift up Jesus and present him as the Good News that he is.

+No Western or Christian Culture. You are witnessing to Jesus, not Western culture. Don't confuse the two. He writes,

We teach who we are. You can see it in different kinds of churches too. Some churches are sure they have to speak loudly with great animation for God to hear. Others are obviously convinced that God can reach the mind because you will never hear a peep from them. Some raise hands. Others bend knees. Some preachers shout for an hour while others memorize a ten-minute homily. Some dance. Some would never think of moving. Hard benches. Soft chairs. Choirs. Rock bands. Steeples and stained glass. And some even think they can meet God in homes. And what's funny is they all back up their cultures with scripture. (p. 160-161)

Carl has a list of 21 do's and don'ts. They actually boil down to this—care enough about Muslims that you don't act in ways they would experience as rude or offensive. This means getting to know a little about their culture, such as what they do with respect to alcohol, pork, touching someone, modest dress, respecting the Quran and the prophets, praying with them, etc.

Don't assume you know what a Muslim believes. Ask questions and learn about them from them. Share your story and yourself. Be a friend.

So, would you see Carl's "model" as a form of friendship evangelism, or contextualization, or both? What do you think his view is about the confrontational model? Is he describing a combination of models? Does he advocate a new model? These are important thoughts and discussions to have with those who would like to reach out to Muslims.

George Houssney

I consider George a friend, and I truly appreciate many aspects of his approach to reaching out to Muslims. You will note that it has both similarities and differences from Carl's approach. On the essentialism-nominalism continuum, George would be more toward the essentialism end of the pole than Carl or I would be. His wonderful book, Engaging Islam, has a chapter on the Arab character of Islam in which he describes the "Arab Character" which he sees as constitutive of the worldview within the Qur'an and hadith. In still another chapter he covers what he calls the "Muslim identity." These are clearly essentialist ventures and while I tend more toward nominalism, I find George's discussions interesting and informative if understood as broad brush strokes rather than a detailed description of each Muslim's identity devoid of each person's uniqueness. If wrongly understood, these chapters could tend toward a cookie cutter approach to Muslims, but that in no way is George's approach. His approach is nuanced and sensitive.

In chapter nine entitled, "When You Meet a Muslim," and chapter ten, "The Art of Asking Questions" one can clearly see how George's loving approach does indeed focus on the uniqueness of a Muslim. The advice that he gives in chapter nine is as follows:

+**Seek out opportunities to witness to Muslims**. If you aren't naturally around Muslims, you are not absolved of reaching out to them. Be proactive and take the initiative.
+**Pray for opportunities** to engage Muslims
+**Seize opportunities**, which is to say that when you do meet a Muslim, reach out with the love of Jesus
+**The battle is in the heart**. George clearly believes that in an interaction with a Muslim there comes a moment when the discussion needs to become very personal and focus on the basic longing of the Muslim's heart which is the security of the Muslim's eternal destiny. Don't miss the moment.
+**Offer hospitality and friendship**. Many Muslim students come to the United States to study, and the majority is never invited to an American's home. These are missed opportunities to show hospitality and friendship to a Muslim. George points out that the majority of Muslims who come to the Lord do so in part through the hospitality and friendship of a Christian.

+Use the Bible. Here George shows his boldness. He says that when people ask him whether to give the Bible to a Muslim he says, "Yes, what else are you going to give him? A Qur'an. A Buddha? Give him a Bible!" (p. 122). There is power in the Word and its message of salvation. Share it.

+Tell the story of the Gospel. The message is simple and can very simply be shared. Do not make it complicated by being overly abstract. Abstractions do not move the heart. Tell the Gospel story through your story.

+Deal with one person at a time. Witnessing to a Muslim in the presence of Muslim peers may simply be counterproductive. It is vitally important to focus on one person and that person's questions. No Muslims wants to appear as though she or he is interested in Christianity in front of her/his friends or family.

+Do not invite Muslims to church until they are ready—home groups are often better. Many of us know the story of Sayyid Qutb who was a student from Egypt to the United States in the 1940s. He visited a church and when he saw the free mingling of the sexes in the church during a dance, he was horrified. He returned to Egypt and wrote a vitriolic book, <u>Milestones,</u> condemning the West and became a key figure in the Muslim Brotherhood, an organization that many view as the spiritual forefathers of radical expressions of Islam. Some Christians in a church may make some very negative and unloving remarks about Muslims in the presence of a Muslim visitor, which would be counterproductive.

+Do not argue. We tend to argue about ideas and doctrine, not story. Thus George relies heavily on story. Rather than debate, share your story.

+Pray!

+Share current answers to prayers. Let Muslims see how God is working in your life.

+Give more literature, videos and Bibles. This recommendation stems from George's belief that there is a strong positive correlation between the distribution of Christian literature and the conversion of Muslims.

+Work as a team. Increase the number of good Christians experienced by a Muslim.
+Be persistent. Engaging Muslims can be frustrating. Engaging anyone can be frustrating. Work through the frustration and be persistent.

In addition to the above list, George advocates asking Muslims personal probing questions. The bottom line is to ask personal questions and then be quiet and listen carefully to what the Muslim says. Don't ask about Islam or the Qur'an so much as about the Muslim personally and her/his life. Be ready to receive difficult questions from Muslims. Be honest if you don't have an answer. Say, "I don't know." Be ready to answer the question in a helpful way. For example, if the Muslim asks about the Trinity, feel free to respond with something such as "to understand that we need to ask a more basic question" and then proceed to discuss the more basic issue.

Share experiences such as movies or television shows and use them as occasions to ask questions. Be curious!

I hope you have noticed that the major models that were presented, along with the models of Carl Medearis and George Houssney, are quite different and yet have some important similarities. For example, one might notice that the confrontational approach of Jay Smith and the non-confrontational approach of Carl Medearis both involve deep connections with Muslims. Jay's approach may be marked by disputation, but the context in which that occurs is deeply relational. The relational element of Carl's approach is obvious. Then there are the multiple expressions of contextualization vis-a-vis the approach of George Houssney, which very much seems anti-contextual. And yet, both approaches are deeply relational. I can't help but wonder if we took the time to study all these models and the instances in which they were successful, whether we would find that the relational element is pivotal to the positive outcome. It has not been adequately studied to my knowledge, and so we can't know for certain. I know some evangelicals say that it is all about relationship. However, this needs to be verified empirically. I hope some bright graduate student takes this on as a dissertation topic and begins to bring to light the relative importance of all the elements that make up each model. This might be more profitable than generating untested models all claiming to be grounded in scripture. It could well be that all are indeed grounded in scripture. If so, that is deeply instructive, but it needs to be verified empirically.

Chapter 7--Is There a Jesus Model?

Little children, let us not love in word or speech but in deed and in truth.—I John 3:18

Every model for reaching out to Muslims claims to be grounded in scripture and yet often these models contain contradictory recommendations and approaches. If we truly followed the way of Jesus even in a way that tries to duplicate how Jesus interacted with others, what would that look like? How would we act? What exactly would we do? Would we spend the bulk of our time quoting Torah to Muslims? Probably not. Jesus often alluded to Torah or even quoted it, but he did much more than quote Torah.

Would we spend the bulk of our time debating? Probably not. Jesus rarely debated and when he was argumentative, it was often with those who already embraced the truth, or claimed to do so, but who didn't live it and missed the heart of an authentic faith.

What should we do?

Well, I am told that over 60% of what Jesus said was in the form of stories or parables. He told great stories that captured the minds and hearts of the hearers of those stories. We still find deep meaning and relevance in them centuries later. So I guess we would tell stories—a lot of stories.

We would probably hang out with people in good times and bad times. We would go to parties and do what we could to make those parties even more fun (within reason)—the whole water to wine episode. That kept the party going and at the same time showed who he really was at the same time. We would go the homes of those who had experienced tragedy, such as the death of a loved one. We would end up comforting them after sharing their pain. In so doing, we would be pointing to the real Resurrection.

We would meet people as they did their chores in the midst of emotional pain. I guess we would enter into the lives of others to the extent that we knew their pain and we would touch that pain.

We would hang out with those rejected by "respectable society"—people with unmentionable jobs and diseases not talked about in polite settings. We wouldn't worry too much what those in power, or what those who are the arbiters of acceptable culture thought.

We would make sure that everyone had something to eat and drink. We would make sure that they had necessary health care (I am not getting political here or taking sides in silly political debates). I am just noting what the one I love did from day to day.

We would go to church but would do so without being "churchy." We would take religious rituals and traditions and give them new meaning in ways that help people see that the Kingdom of God is right here and needs to be celebrated.

We would work alongside people and help them see the greater work God has called them to do—the whole fishers of men, women, and children vocation.

We would care about our neighbor and see that our neighbor is everyone in the world. We would be light years beyond nationalism and see the value of everyone in every culture—like a Samaritan who looked beyond labels to see a fellow human in need.

We would help others overcome their view of themselves as irreparably damaged or victims for life—we would help them pick up their mat and get to work helping others and themselves. We would go to great lengths to help them get the care they need—remember how people lowered a man through a roof to make sure he got helped by Jesus?

We would thank people for inadvertently, but actually, helping us in the context of them helping others in need—Day of Judgment scene with the sheep and the goats.

If there is a clear simple model for reaching out to Muslims that is confined only to what Jesus did, I guess it would include all the elements I just mentioned. I am not suggesting that if Jesus were here today that he would do only these things, but what he did while on earth should be instructive for us today.

Whatever models we develop should be informed by these actions. Better still, what if we put our energy more into living like Jesus than in forming models and strategies for reaching Muslims? What if we entered their lives, not in the abstract but through concrete healing and transformative words and actions? I am not suggesting that we refrain from model building or testing the efficacy of those models. I think we actually should be far more rigorous than we are about testing models and methods. Part of my frustration with us Christians who say that we are deeply interested in missions work is that for something so important we are so lazy in scrutinizing our ways and submitting them to rigorous scientific standards. However, beneath the models, stats, tests, tactics, strategies, etc., we need to be inspired by a huge vision that is the life of Jesus and what he did day to day with those who knew neither him nor the Kingdom of God.

Let me muddy the water a little here. I think that we Christians often fall somewhere along a universal-contingent continuum. Both love God and the Word, but we approach it in ways that we tend to make fairly predictable mistakes in determining what God would have us do. There are several ways to characterize this spectrum. I choose to do it in terms of how individuals determine universals. There are those who have a tendency to look at seeming universals and deny their universality (the universal deniers), and then there are those who look at contingent realities/situations and declare them to be universals (the universal multipliers). I think both are guilty of what I call "the fallacy of the misplaced universal."

Universal deniers tend to read scripture and for what seems to be a verse that is making a universal appeal, they tend to read it as a contingent appeal. For example, when Jesus says to love our neighbor as our self, the universal denier would see the statement as contingent on whether the individual is an enemy or not, a Christian or not, etc. The universal multiplier would tend to read a seemingly contingent passage and declare it to be universal.

For example, consider Acts 17 in which Paul argues with the philosophers and others at the Areopagus in Athens, all pagans. The universal multipliers read this exchange and declare that arguing with non-believers is "the way" to interact with nonbelievers, i.e., arguing with nonbelievers is a universal. The reason I consider such approaches as instances of the fallacy of the misplaced universal is that the verses are superficially read and there is no clear method delineated for determining the presence or absence of a universal. I think this often happens with respect to the models we develop for reaching Muslims. We read a passage and either declare it to be a universal or not, when what we might better do is to determine whether we are logically justified in determining the presence or absence of a universal. Perhaps God is calling us to know something about the ones with whom we are interacting, know the truth we want to share, and then determine through reason and the life example of Jesus, as well as studying and research, the most effective way, or ways, to reach this particular group or this particular person. Perhaps the true universal is arrived at through that process of considering reality in light of the life example of Jesus and detailed research. Sure, it is more work than just reading the scripture and declaring that we are absolutely certain that we have fully grasped the one and only way. The trouble with this latter approach is that there are so many people embracing conflicting ways and all declaring that they have "the way" and all arguing against the other "wrongheaded ways." I think the matter is serious enough to work a little more and to be a little more humble about having "the way."

Chapter 8--Special Muslim Populations, Special Problems

Jesus helped those who suffered and he continues to do so directly as well as indirectly through us. We need to cooperate with him and help Muslims who suffer. In this chapter I will focus on two populations of Muslims who suffer emotionally and in other ways. Pray and see whether God is calling you to cooperate with him and fellow Christians to help these special populations of Muslims.

Refugees

In 2009 it was estimated that 40% of the refugees to the United States come from Muslim countries (Ahmed & Amer, 281). Ahmed and Aboul-Fotouh (282) discuss the phases of the migratory process and the issues in each phase. As you encounter Muslim refugees in Western countries it is helpful to find out what their migratory situation was like. Refugees with higher levels of education are often better able to understand their current refugee situation and form a plan to adjust to the new situations. Those with less education may need greater levels of professional mental health assistance and more ongoing financial assistance and help navigating through social services. Christian groups can be invaluable helping these individuals with these very concrete issues.

Muslims seeking asylum can be missing necessary paper documentation of their identity. It would be normal for them to feel lost, hopeless, angry, fearful, distrustful, powerless, and out of control. Knowing safe individuals to talk to and support them can be very helpful.

Their problems are numerous and groups of Christians, Christian organizations, or groups acting collaboratively can address some of their challenges, such as housing, health care, education, language acquisition, employment, social support, and adjusting to the new culture.

Converts to Islam

Many Christians feel sad and disappointed, or even angry, when they hear about a Christian who has converted to Islam. Often the Christian feels as though she/he and the church have totally and irreversibly failed because they think of conversion in inadequate ways. They assume conversion is a linear and clear process that tends to be irreversible. However, conversion isn't linear; it isn't irreversible; and it is not a clear all-or-nothing process. It is more often than not an ambiguous process with a long phase of uncertainty of identity—a rather fluid process. The conversion process can be joyous but is more often than not quite stressful. Research into converts to Islam has noted the following:

+Many converts describe the early years after conversion as "tumultuous" with many highs and lows
+They experience challenges adjusting to their new faith, especially with issues associated with family, friends, and dealing with Islamophobia
+Some converts join Islamic organizations that help with their adjustment
+Some converts succumb to the stressors and leave Islam.
+Some converts have difficulty with their new faith's prohibitions against dating and the difficulties surrounding finding a suitable spouse.
+Some converts experience the stressors associated with a cross-cultural marriage.
+Some converts experience isolation and loneliness due to factors such as language and culture.
+Some converts experience difficulties finding new leisure activities that don't involve alcohol, drugs, or mingling with those of the opposite sex.
+Some converts experience stressors in change of diet, sleep schedules, prayer times, as well as praying and worshiping in a foreign language. (Ahmed, 229-250)

Christians who can be with converts and listen to them talk about their stressors without criticizing Islam and thereby forcing the convert to defend his/her faith can be invaluable. I was at a conference of Muslim background believers (MBBs) that was visited by a recent convert to Islam. A small group of MBBs became so excited that they gathered around the convert, lay hands on her, and offered a long series of prayers that contained criticisms of Islam. I had the chance to talk to this young lady when the group stopped and just as she was getting ready to leave. She said that it was this kind of insensitivity that was the reason she left the church and the actions of these well-meaning MBBs that convinced her that her conversion was the right thing to do. I have no doubt that the MBBs meant well, but they lacked wisdom and judgment. I never found out what brought this young convert to Islam to this particular conference and I am sure that not one of the MBBs took the time to listen to her and find out what was on her heart. Sad. I know that some of you may be thinking that they were just trying to seize the opportunity. That is the problem. They focused on the opportunity rather than the precious young Muslim convert in front of them.

This is a natural segue into the next chapter in which I consider the ways in which we Christians sabotage our efforts to reach Muslims.

Chapter 9--How Not to Sabotage Your Efforts to Reach Muslims

For as he thinketh in his heart so is he—Proverbs 23:7

Nearly every book I have read that was written by a Christian about how to reach Muslims tends to focus on the Muslim—understanding the Muslim mind, a particular Muslim ethnic population or culture, misunderstandings Muslims have about the Bible or Christian beliefs, or what to do and not to do with Muslims and the challenges involved in doing so. Rarely do I see anything written about the Christian and how the Christian may sabotage her/his efforts. That makes sense. It is much easier to externalize a problem than to look within the self. Jesus addressed this tendency when he said,

Why do you see the speck that is in your brother's eye, but do not notice the log that is in your own eye? Or how can you say to your brother, Let me take the speck out of your eye, when there is the log in your own eye? You hypocrite, first take the log out of your own eye, and then you will see clearly to take the speck out of your brother's eye. (Matthew 7:3-5)

Jesus sternly tells us not to externalize problems before we look at the most obvious problems--, you, me-- who see faults in others. My hypothesis is that I am my greatest obstacle in reaching out to Muslims. You are your greatest obstacle. That is not fun to hear, but I actually think it is good news. Jesus is clear that we have the capacity to change that tendency to externalize problems and find the obstacles within ourselves. That is fantastic news. This chapter covers one aspect of how to do just that. I have done workshops on this for years and invariably there are some people in attendance who want to argue and say that Muslims are the problem. Again, that is natural, but the reality is that the Muslim is just being a Muslim doing what that particular Muslim does. If we experience that as a problem, then we really

71

have a problem because the world and others are not always the way we would like them to be. That is the context in which we are to reach out to Muslims, so we have to deal with it and scrutinize ourselves and determine whether we are thinking, feeling, and acting in ways that sabotage us in this effort. That is what I want to cover in this chapter. If you find yourself getting a little nervous about what I say, just know that this is normal and can be worked through. It is all a part of growing in the Lord.

Proverbs 23:7 reads, "For as a man thinks in his heart so is he." That means that our emotions and our behaviors are caused largely by the way we think. That means that we are responsible for our emotions and behaviors. We can't legitimately blame people, circumstances, situations, or even mom and dad for how we feel and act. The good news is that we can change the way we think. Is it easy? Usually not, but it is possible.

My assumption is that we often sabotage ourselves in our efforts to reach out to Muslims as a result of our unhelpful emotions and behaviors as we interact with them. The Proverbs 23:7 verse suggests that these emotions and behaviors are largely caused by our thoughts or beliefs. Again, that is good news because we can change those thoughts and beliefs—if we are honest with ourselves about our real thoughts, we actively work at changing those thoughts, and we ask for God's help in doing so.

What are some unhelpful or self-sabotaging emotions and behaviors?
+Unhelpful emotions: anger/rage, high frustration, anxiety, depression, fear
+Unhelpful behaviors: argumentativeness, avoidance, dwelling on the negative, aggression, pushiness, rudeness, defensiveness, blaming, prejudicial statements

Some of you might be thinking that some of these are normal emotions and behaviors in some circumstances. Perhaps, but I think that is the wrong focus. A question to pose to you is "Are these emotions and behaviors helpful in reaching Muslims?" You may be normal or even justified in your emotions and behaviors, but end up ruining relationships. How is that helpful?

I am reminded of I Corinthians 8 in which Paul considers the permissibility of Christians eating meat sacrificed to idols. The bottom line is that while it is perfectly permissible theologically and in practice, it may not be helpful to exercise that freedom in the presence of a Christian who would be troubled by us doing so. Similarly, while we may be justified in our emotions and our behaviors, the important question is whether they are helpful to others or to us.

Below are some thoughts that we may have that set the stage for our unhelpful emotions and self-sabotaging behaviors:

+**Demanding kinds of thoughts:** these thoughts often contain words such as 'should', 'ought',' must',' have to', or 'need'.
++I must not make a mistake when I witness to a Muslim
++Muslims should not criticize the Bible or my faith.
++It shouldn't be so difficult to reach out with the truth.
++I should only have to be concerned with telling a Muslim the truth, not with how I tell the truth
++Fellow Christians must agree with me in how to reach out to Muslims
++I must correct a Muslim when she/he says something about my faith that isn't true.
+**"I can't stand it" kinds of thoughts**
++I can't stand it when a Muslim attacks my faith or criticizes the Bible.
++I can't stand being around Muslims who aren't open to the truth
++I can't stand Muslims who criticize Israel or the United States
++I can't stand liberal Christians who only want to have dialogue with Muslims
+**"This is awful" kinds of thoughts**
+It is awful when Muslims can't see the truth of the Bible
+It is awful when Christians don't agree with me about how to reach out to Muslims
+**'All,' 'always,' or 'never' kinds of thoughts**
++A devout Muslim will never leave her/his faith

++All Muslims hate Christians and Christianity
++Muslims will never be open to the truth.
++Muslims will never be peace-loving
+Other downing—globally putting someone else down
++Muslims are ignorant rejecters of the truth
++Other Christians are stupid when they don't agree with me about how to reach out to Muslims
++Muslims are terrorists by nature

Of course, this list is not exhaustive. I am sure you have heard, and maybe have even uttered, other unhelpful kinds of thoughts. It is even possible to combine these unhelpful kinds of thoughts into larger unhelpful thoughts. An example is, "Christians must agree with me about how to reach out to Muslims, and they are misguided or stupid if they don't."

One of the problems with this kind of thinking is that it causes us to experience emotions that don't help us in interacting with Muslims or even our fellow Christians. Another problem is that they are so prideful, i.e., they set us up as the judge of others and assume that we are noble enough for that office. A bigger problem is that they tend to be grounded in idolatry. To hold demanding kinds of thoughts assumes that others and situations must be the way I want them to be. Why? Because I want them to be that way or because I am a representative of God and you must agree with me as such.

To believe that I can't stand something is to give ultimate power over me to a situation or person. There is only one being that should have that level of power in my life, and that is God. Paul realized the folly of the "I can't stand this" kind of thinking when he wrote,

"For I have learned to find resources in myself whatever my circumstances" (Philippians 4:11).

The same for believing that something is awful in the sense of destroying all meaning, purpose, or joy in my life. If I

74

truly believe in God and hold fast to the truth, then there is nothing that is awful in that total sense. Sure, there are bad situations in life and major tragedies, but nothing can have such power as to totally destroy meaning, purpose, or joy.

To put someone else down is to deny their intrinsic value and to inflate our own value. We have no right to put others down globally. This is to implicitly deny that the other person is created in the image of God and that Christ died for them, which is witness to the value that God gives to each of us—all of us. Sure, we are a mess, but that is true of all of us as humans. There are no exceptions.

The 'always' and 'never' kind of thinking is what I call "false prophecy." We act as though we have the knowledge of God to be able to declare what others will do in the future. This kind of thinking denies that each of us is created with free will.

All these unhelpful ways of thinking are grounded in attributing the power and knowledge of God to the self, or to give God-like power to something other than God. That is the very nature of idolatry. We need to let God be God and work to rid the self of such kind of thinking. Is it any wonder that this kind of thinking sabotages us in life in general and in reaching out to Muslims?

A year ago, I lectured to a group of Christians who allegedly were interested in reaching out to Muslims in the area. I was covering some of the material in this book, when a lady interrupted me and said, "The trouble with you is that you are more loving toward Muslims than Jesus was." This individual's method of reaching out to Muslims was to go to a Dunkin' Donut store that was frequented by Muslims on Saturday morning. She would stand outside the building and hold signs condemning Islam and Muslims and ask them to accept Jesus. In a conversation with her later, she told me that she thought that those Muslims were given a chance to accept Jesus and that they should have done it right then and there or they were going to hell. Of course, no Muslims accepted Jesus in those settings. I explored a few of her other unhelpful beliefs and then asked what she really felt about Muslims. She was very honest and said, "I hate Muslims. They should all go back to their own country." Now this is an extreme example, but it shows how unhelpful actions and emotions are grounded in unhelpful thoughts. I wonder what her emotions and behaviors would have been if she thought, "I wish these precious Muslims would come to know Jesus, but whether they do or don't, I am going to reflect the love of Christ to them as much as I am able." She might have been somewhat disappointed and sad that the Muslims didn't come to the Lord, but I doubt that she would hate them and shout that hatred in word and on signs. Please do not hear me as hating this lady or putting her down. She is no different than any of us. We all have our areas about which we hold unhelpful beliefs and it shows in our emotions and behaviors. Praise God, we can change!

In Oevures de Descartes one finds the famous quote of Rene Descartes, the famous philosopher:

Suppose [a person] had a basket full of apples and, being worried that some of the apples were rotten, wanted to take out the rotten ones to prevent the rot spreading. How would he proceed? Would he not begin by tipping the whole lot out of the basket? And would not the next step be to cast his eye over each apple in turn, and pick up and put back in the basket only those he saw to be sound, leaving the others? In just the same way, those who have never philosophized correctly have various opinions in their minds which they have begun to store up since childhood, and which they therefore have reason to believe may in many cases be false. They then attempt to separate the false beliefs from the others, so as to prevent their contaminating the rest and making the whole lot uncertain. Now the best way they can accomplish this is to reject all their beliefs together in one go, as if they were all uncertain and false. They can then go over each belief in turn and re-adopt only those which they recognize to be true and indubitable.

I am not advocating the method of methodological doubt that Descartes proposes, but he was onto something important. I think that as Christians we should examine our thoughts and make sure that they glorify God or lead to actions that glorify God. If they don't, then we need to change them or eliminate them.

So what can we do with these unhelpful thoughts?

+Ask God to make such unhelpful thoughts evident to you.

+Enlist the help of other sensitive Christians to help identify these thoughts in us.

+Pray for help to change the thoughts.

+Use scripture to replace these thoughts with more helpful thoughts grounded in godly desires.

+Use a journal as a place to identify the unhelpful thoughts and to argue against them, i.e., show their inadequacy and replace them with helpful thoughts.

+When you are talking to a Muslim and you become aware of any unhelpful emotions and behaviors, stop and shift to a prayer. Let the Muslim know that you are going to take a few seconds to pray for him/her and you. Actually, this is a great way to handle conflict too.

+Do not model your interactions with Muslims after Christians who act upon unhelpful thoughts yielding unhelpful emotions and behaviors. Model yourself after Christ and those who show his love for others, including Muslims.

In psychotherapy there is a distinction made between content and process. Content is what is said; process is how it is said along with associated body language. This is another way to say what rhetorical theory says about an argument or message. In apologetics, content is the focus rather than the process. This is fine if we are narrowly looking at the logical adequacy of a message, but if we are concerned about persuasion of real humans who have emotions and are influenced by the quality of a relationship, then we should probably broaden our scope and become very curious about process.

While interacting with Muslims isn't psychotherapy, the distinction between process and content can be helpful. Make sure the content of what you say is truthful and logical and listen very carefully to the content of the Muslim's message. However, be aware of the process between the two of you or between you and the audience. Be aware of the following:

+How you are feeling emotionally
+How the Muslim seems to be feeling emotionally
+Your body language and actions
+The body language and action of the Muslims
+What thoughts you are having about the Muslim, yourself, what is happening between the two of you, etc.?
+What prejudices or biases are getting triggered in you?

Let me give an example of something that happened to me that highlights the process-content distinction. Nearly everyone at church knew I was trying to lose some weight and most people were wonderfully supportive of my efforts. One Sunday, however, a lady approached me saying, "It looks as though you are failing at your diet?" Immediately I noticed that I was confused, annoyed, if not angry with what I heard. I became aware of my thoughts:

+She shouldn't have said this to me
+How awful that she said this
+What a rude insensitive person she is; she should give me credit for how hard I am working at this rather than making fun of me.

Fortunately, instead of just reacting to the content of her statement and the unhelpful thoughts in my head, I tried to counter those messages in my head and decided to shift from content to process with respect to the communication between us. When I made that shift, I was able to say, "That felt like an attack. Was that what you intended to do?" She nervously laughed and said that this was not her intention, but that she was just trying to be funny. I said, "I am so glad I asked you. I guess I am being oversensitive to the whole diet thing right now." She apologized, we laughed, talked about how difficult diets can be. We left knowing each other better and feeling safe to share more in the future. Shifting from content to process can be tough and so can changing our unhelpful beliefs to helpful ones, but the work is well worth it. Shifting focus is extremely important as a Christian. This fact is very powerfully made by Paul in II Corinthians 4:16-18 when he tells us that we can keep from losing hope if we shift our focus in the following way:

+Realize that whatever we are going through is not huge, but merely a "slight momentary affliction." So, don't treat the issue or circumstance as huge.

+Shift your attention away from the drama in front of you to eternal truths, such as "nothing can separate us from the love of God," "God loves both the Muslim in front of me and me," etc.

We see some other good advice modeled in Lamentations 3:1-21. In verses 1-19 we get a long list of symptoms of depression experienced by Jeremiah along with some of his unhelpful thoughts that are causing those symptoms. Then in verse 20, we get the secret to his misery when he says, "my soul continually thinks on this day and night." Yes, that is the secret to misery. Rather than thinking negative and unhelpful thoughts once or just a few times, focus on them repeatedly. But Jeremiah doesn't stay stuck in his depression. He shifts his thinking away from unhelpful thinking to quite helpful thinking as in the following verses:

But this I call to mind, and therefore I have hope: The steadfast love of the Lord never ceases, his mercies never come to an end: they are new every morning; great is they faithfulness. (Lamentations 3: 21-23)

Perfect! We can shift our attention from negative thinking to logical realistic thinking, and we can shift from content to process. The reality is that there is perhaps more meaning in how we say something than in what we say. Content is extremely important, but so much emotion is attached to the process and these emotions can help people accept or reject, trust or mistrust the content.

I learned this when I was a new father. My daughter was about 3 and was dressed up like a pumpkin for Halloween. She was so excited that she ran down the driveway, slipped, and scraped her knee. I ran to her trying to say some words to take away the pain, but in the next few seconds, she taught me the difference between process and content, the difference between a message and how a message is packaged. She said, "Daddy, no words, just hugs!" So many verses in the Bible have us relate to God and God relate to us beyond words, verses such as "taste and see the goodness of the Lord," "our heart cries out for the living God," "rest in the Lord," etc. Process! Content is vital to knowing the truth, but God is equally about process. That is what it means to be a child, parent, spouse, believer, friend to a Muslim, to any human. We listen to the words and we pay attention to how they are said, as well as the emotion surrounding them.

Chapter 10--Please Don't Do This To A Muslim!

I thought on my ways and turned my feet.—Psalm 119:59

I didn't think a book written by a Christian about reaching out to Muslims would be complete without a few "Thou shalt not's."

+**Don't** tell a Muslim what she/he believes. Don't state as fact what you think all Muslims believe, or what the Qur'an really means.

+**Don't** tell a Muslim that the origin of Allah is the worship of a moon god. You are talking to a Muslim who does not believe in a moon good and probably never did. This is just weird and rude.

+**Don't** argue over whether Muslims believe in the same God as Christians do. I know that theologians live for these kinds of issues, and as a philosopher, I can spend hours stretched out on a couch pondering issues like this. Ok, let's allow my inner philosopher to kick into action and say that as a philosopher the issue is: how many necessary characteristics of God do we have to believe in to believe in the true God? How many wrong characteristics can we believe in and still believe in the true God? I guess we could list the necessary and sufficient conditions or traits an entity must have to be the true God. Then one could compare an individual or group's list of traits attributed to God to determine whether their list is comprised of those necessary and sufficient characteristics or traits. I guess a further question is whether one can believe in the true God but be confused about the true and complete nature of that God? These are interesting questions and important ones theologically and philosophically, but they aren't appropriate in a discussion with a Muslim. What we can be sure about is that most Muslims don't believe that Jesus is the Lord and Savior, or a person in the Trinity. Rather than debate all the questions above, why not just try to point Muslims to Jesus and do so in inviting and loving ways. There is a huge difference in acting like a philosopher or theologian and being a real person interested in reaching out to the mind and heart of a Muslim.

+**Don't** insult Muhammad. That is like telling someone that their mother is a prostitute or their father is a pedophile. That is probably not a great way to form a friendship. It isn't going to work unless the individual really hates his/her mother or father. You have probably heard how this has sparked some unfortunate events throughout the world. Why go there? What is it about you that would even have you want to go there?

+**Don't** describe Islam as a form of works righteousness. Muslims tend to believe that getting to heaven is contingent on both right belief and right action. I guess that makes it a form of faith-works righteousness.

+**Don't** tell Muslims what the Qur'an says. The Qur'an is interpreted and has been interpreted in many different ways. I don't like for Muslims to tell me what the Bible "really" says and they are no different about the Qur'an. It is better to ask the Muslims what she/he thinks a Qur'anic passage means.

+**Don't** assume that you know what Muslims are like. Muslims are unique individuals. Talk to them; get to know them. Reading a recipe for a chocolate cake is worlds away from taking that first bite. Reading all the creeds written by the church over the centuries is worlds away from having a relationship with Jesus. Instead of reading about Muslims and thinking that you understand Muslims; talk to a Muslim. I know, right now you are reading a book about Muslims, but at some point you will close this book and at that point, my hope is that you become informed about the Muslim who is in front of you by your experience of that Muslims.

+**Don't** assume that all Muslim women experience themselves as oppressed. Many converts to Islam in the West are upper middle class educated Caucasian women who say that they have experienced liberation within Islam and by wearing hijab. You may see it differently or be baffled how this could be, but that is what many claim. Get a grip on your prejudice or preconceptions.

+**Don't** assume that Muslims are empty vessels into which you need to pour knowledge. Muslims are bright valuable people too. They have minds and the ability to reason. Many think deeply about their faith and are curious about your faith. Interact with them without being condescending or treating them as though they are little children.

+**Don't** interact with Muslims as if you are a professor giving a lecture, as if you know it all, as though they are a project, as if they are an object for your outreach strategy, or as if they are exotic creatures. Be real and let them be real.

Chapter 11--Conclusion

When I was in graduate school, I had a philosophy professor who was not only the best professor I ever had, but one of the most humble human beings I have been blessed to know. The first course I had with him was an evening course in value theory that was scheduled from 5:30 to 8 pm with a 15 minute break somewhere near the middle of the class. Typically, the class went from 5:30 to 9:30, most often without a break. At the end of every class he did the same thing. He would chuckle lightly and then say, "But I could be all wrong."

I loved that humble admission of fallibility from a world class philosopher. I have tried to take that attitude into my faith, and it has really helped my spiritual growth. For example, I believe the Word of God is infallible, but I know that my interpretation of that Word is not. I try to remind myself of that reality as often as possible. I believe the Church is the Body of Christ and thereby stamped with divinity in some way, and yet it is made up of fallible messed up humans, and I am one of them. My best friend is Roman Catholic and jokes, "If 2,000 years of priests have not been able to destroy the church, it must be the truth church." That joke contains a lot of truth about all churches and everyone who attends those churches.

Some people have trouble with the gulf between the perfection of God and the imperfection of God's representatives on earth. Many Muslims are scandalized by the way in which the Bible portrays the prophets as sinners. I actually love it that they are shown for the fragile messed up people that they were. For me it is part of the proof of the truthfulness of scripture. Only God would portray us as we really are. We humans tend to clean up the stories of our heroes. It also gives me hope that God can use me for something worthwhile. Look at it, God chose to use the following:

+A totally dysfunctional family to start the entire human race, knowing that they were going to make a mess for all of us

+A ragtag group of people who couldn't find their way out of the desert and then declared them "Chosen"

+A wild and wooly guy who ate bugs with honey to usher in the ministry of Jesus

+A hotheaded fisherman who chopped off the ear of an enemy to help lead a church that eventually would have over a billion members

+A Mensa type overachiever rabbi who persecuted Christians to become the architect of the Body of Christ and major author of a big chunk of the Bible

+A highly anxious avoidant man with an anger disorder to preach so well that a whole city converted after which this angry guy sat in the sun and pouted

+A group of women, at that time second class members of society, to be the first ones to get evidence of the greatest miracle in history--Prostitutes, cripples, lepers, the blind, the deaf, the dead, the despised, the enemy, the lost, the despairing, the possessed, the mentally ill, thieves, pretty much all kinds of broken people to be major characters in the greatest story ever told....

If God can use them, God can use you and me. We don't have to have it all together, and it is a good thing because we never will. So we can't legitimately say that we don't have what it takes to reach out to Muslims. Why not? Because it doesn't depend on what we have, but on the fact that God made us and called us to do it just as we are, the mess that we are. It is not what we have; it is what he gives us.

Rumi, one of the great Sufi poets, wrote, "the crack is where the light enters." That is beautiful. Paul said it in a different way in II Corinthians 4:7. In that verse Paul calls us earthen vessels, items that are fragile and liable to being broken, not to put us down, but to reframe our fragility and tendency to be broken as an asset because through that fragility, the transcendent power and beauty of God is made evident to others. If we weren't fallible, imperfect, and broken, God's power might not be so visible in the world that has trouble seeing reality for what it is. We demonstrate God's magnificence through the contrast with our fragile nature. So God continues to use a motley crew to get the job done. This is good news. It means that you and I clearly have the skill set for the job.

It deeply pains me when I hear Christians say hateful things about Muslims (and vice versa). It reminds me of what to me is one of the saddest scenes in the Bible. Jonah is sitting in the sun outside the city limits of Ninevah, a city filled with people Jonah hates. As Jonah looks down on the ones he hates, and as he is filled with an anger at God that is so deep that he wants to die, he suffers, wanting nothing but for God to change His mind and kill the Ninevites.

I don't want Christians to be like that with Muslims. I hope that we remember that when God looked down at the Ninevites, He was just rejoicing that the lost were now saved. God is looking down at the Muslims, loving them and wanting us to show that love to those precious Muslims.

References

Adams, C. and Tannery, P. (Eds.). (1904). Oeuvres de Descartes. Paris: J. Vrin.

Ahmed, S. (2012). Converts to Islam. S. Ahmed and M. Amer (Eds.), Counseling Muslims: Handbook of Mental Health Issues and Interventions (pp. 229-250). New York, NY: Routledge.

Ahmed, S and Aboul-Fotouh, F. (2012). Refugees. S. Ahmed and M. Amer (Eds.), Counseling Muslims: Handbook of Mental Health Issues and Interventions (pp. 281-305). New York, NY: Routledge.

Al-Faruqi, I. (1986). Islamic Da'wah Its Nature and Demands. Indianapolis, IN. American Trust Publications.

Baagil, J. (n.d.). Christian Muslim Dialogue. Retrieved from http://www.muslimaccess.com/islamic_resources/muslim_christian_dialogue.htm.

Badawi, J. (n.d.). Jesus in the Qur'an and Bible. Retrieved from http://www.institutealislam.com/jesus-in-the-quran-and-bible-by-dr-jamal-a-badawi/

Bucaille, M. (1977). The Bible, The Qur'an, and Science. Indianapolis, IN: American Trust Publications.

Cialdini, R. (1993). Influence: the Psychology of Persuasion. New York, NY: Quill.

Gilchrist, J. (1999). Facing the Muslim Challenge: A Handbook for Christian-Muslim Apologetics. Cape Town, South Africa: Life Challenge Africa.

Haykal, M. ((1976). The Life of Muhammad. Indianapolis, IN: American Trust Publications.

Houssney, G. (2010). Engaging Islam. Boulder, CO: Treeline Publishing.

Johnson, S. (1989). A Critical Analysis of the Epistemological Basis of ibn Khaldun's Classification of the Sciences. Unpublished doctoral dissertation, Indiana University, Bloomington, IN.

Lucas, G. (Producer), and Spielberg, S. (Director). (1981). Raiders of the Lost Arc [Motion Picture]. United States: Paramount Pictures.

Medearis, C. (2008). Muslims, Christians, and Jesus: Gaining Understanding and Building Relationships. Minneapolis, MN: Bethany House.

Murad, M. (n.d.). The General Prescripts of Belief in the Qur'an and Sunnah. Retrieved from http://www.qss.org/archives/aqeedah/1.html.

Ramage, J, Bean, J, and Johnson, J. (2010). Writing Arguments: A Rhetoric with Readings. New York, NY: Longman.

Terry, M. (1996). Approaches to the Evangelization of Muslims. *Evangelical Missions Quarterly*, 32, 168-173.

Travis, J. (1999). The C1 to C6 Spectrum. In R. Winter and S. Hawthorne (Eds.), Perspectives on the World Christian Movement: A Reader (pp. 658-659). Pasadena, CA: William Carey Library.

Contacting the author

Please feel free to contact the author at
matthew.stone_author@yahoo.com

Made in the USA
San Bernardino, CA
03 October 2014